Understanding Surah Yā-Sīn

Shaykh Muhammad Saeed Bahmanpour

In the Name of God, the Beneficent, the Merciful

Published by Sun Behind The Cloud Publications
PO Box 15889, Birmingham, B16 6NZ

Copyright Mohammad Saeed Bahmanpour © 2018
The moral rights of the author have been reserved
All rights reserved

A CIP catalogue record of this book is available
from the British Library
ISBN (Print): 978-1-908110-50-3
ISBN (eBook): 978-1-908110-51-0

www.sunbehindthecloud.com
info@sunbehindthecloud.com

CONTENTS PAGE

Preface	p5
Introduction	p9
Surah Yā Sīn	p16
Commentary	p 35

PREFACE

Surah Yā Sīn is rightly called the heart of the Qur'ān because it contains the gist of its teachings. If someone wishes to know what the Qur'ān says in a nutshell, they can read Surah Yā Sīn. That is probably the reason it is advised to recite this surah every day so that we do not forget the covenant we have made with God as Muslims.

Surah Yā Sīn teaches us that guidance comes from God, but it is up to us to accept it. It informs us about the story of a community to whom the blessing of guidance was sent, but they turned away from it. This changed their blessing into the curse of ignorance so that they lost focus of the purpose of life and disappeared into the darkness of throwaway civilizations. The surah also reminds us about the blessings around us that we take for granted and the signs of our creator that we have ignored. It talks about the dead earth which comes to life by rain, and the crops that give life to our bodies. It draws our attention to the various elements of the world that he has created, including the sun, the moon, the gardens, the rivers, the fruits and the earth which he has given to us freely and generously.

The surah goes on to educate us about the *purpose* behind these blessings. It teaches us that we are eternal beings: we never perish, travelling from one destination to another until we reach our real home. All the blessings of the world, including the earth itself are merely provisions for the stage of this journey that we spend on the earth. Furthermore, Surah Yā Sīn enlightens us about the last part of this journey; the dramatic stage where every soul realizes that they are either a hostage or a guest of what they have reaped on earth. This is when the whole world dies after the formidable angelic blast, and comes back to life again by the powerful life-spreading second blast. It is after this last stage of the journey that we will find out where our final abode lies, and we will then live either in peace and bliss forever or in agony and pain.

An important covenant is mentioned in this surah. It is an agreement which is installed in our very nature as children of Adam and of which we will be questioned when we meet our Lord. The covenant urges us to be goodly and Godly, and blames us when we pursue evil or follow the devil. The surah ends with a beautiful reminder of the power of God and ignorance of man:

> And he cites an example for us, while forgetting his own creation! He says: "Who can resurrect the bones while they have decayed?" Say: "The one who initiated them in the first place will resurrect them. He has knowledge of all

creation". The one who initiated for you a forest fire by which you learned to light. Is not the one who created the heavens and the earth able to create the like of them? Yes, indeed; he is the All Creator, the All-knowing. All his command, when he wills something, is to say to it, 'Be', and it is. (36:78-81)

Before moving on to the *tafsīr*, a couple of notes should be made here. The present book is as a transcript of my lectures on the *tafsīr* of Surah Yā Sīn, and may lack some features of a pre-planned authored work, above all the style of written books. It further does not contain any references or bibliography. I was contemplating whether to add references while the book was being prepared for publication, but I thought it would be unnecessary and would make the text needlessly complicated for its typical reader.

In most cases I have decided not to capitalise pronouns referring to God; including him, his, we, our, and so on. Although both lower case and capped styles have long and deep-rooted histories in English literature, recent style manuals advocate the use of lower case pronouns in almost all instances. Some find the use of capitals jarring and unnecessary whilst others feel that in English grammar, capitalisation is not used to confer respect. In either case, the aim here is to make the text clear and easy to read.

The complete Surah Yā Sīn in Arabic and English has been rendered below for those who wish the read the surah from start to finish. In the column on the left of the surah are the page numbers which correspond to the commentary of those verses.

The translation of the Holy Qur'ān preferred here is by Ali Quli Qara'i for consistency, even when the commentary discusses other possible readings.

I have to thank Taazeem-Fatemah Esmail, Masserat Alarakhia-Bhanji, Ziana Mawji, and Sumayya Hemraj for producing the transcripts from the recordings. It was a painstaking job due to a mixture of Arabic and English expressions used in the commentary. I am immensely indebted to Tehseen Merali for editing the transcripts. It was like carving a beautiful sculpture out of a rock. I must also thank Zainab Hemani and Zainab Merali for their work in proofreading the book.

May the Lord enlighten our hearts with the light of the Qur'ān and guide us to his path and pleasure.

Mohammad Saeed Bahmanpour
April 2018

INTRODUCTION

Methods of Interpreting the Qur'ān

Before proceeding to start the actual *tafsīr* of the verses, a few points need to be mentioned regarding the method I am using in this commentary.

From the beginning of the revelation, the companions of the Prophet were eager to understand the meanings of verses of the Qur'ān as correctly and accurately as possible. They sought the best methods and tried different approaches to improve their understanding of God's communication. Since the Prophet (s) was the best source for the authentic understanding the Qur'ān, the companions would go directly to the Prophet (s) and ask him about different verses. For instance, they would ask him about how a verse regarding a specific practice like *ṣalāt*, or *zakāt* had to be carried out. The Qur'ān had explicitly assigned the Messenger of God with the duty of explaining its verses to the people around him: 'And we sent down the reminder to you so that you may clarify for the people that which has been sent down to them, so that they may reflect.' (16:44)

After the Prophet passed away, the issue became problematic. The commentators of the Qur'ān disagreed on the meaning of almost every verse, leaving the reader of God's book in confusion. There were reports and counter-reports, views and counter-views, which made attaining a straightforward understanding of the Qur'ān very difficult. Comprehensive *tafāsīr*, such as Tabari's *Jami' al-Bayan* and Ṭabrasī's *Majm' al-Bayaan* reveal the various and opposing opinions of the companions, their successors, and of the later *mufassirīn* regarding the majority of verses.

The Shi'as could have sought explanation from their infallible Imams, but the Imams (as) were not always available, especially to people who were living far away with little means of communication. Thus, the confusion was widespread, both in the Shi'a and Sunni world. This situation urged the need for methods to be available which could produce a reliable interpretation of the Qur'ān in order to understand its true meaning. This is of great importance, as misunderstanding this book, or sometimes even a single verse of it, might affect the whole spiritual, personal and social life of individuals and communities.

Since the narrations of the Prophet and the Imams were scarce, the scholars tried to find other methods of understanding the Qur'ān and establish criteria by which they could judge between different interpretations. As a result, different methods of understanding the Qur'ān were developed. The philosophers developed a rational method, which meant understanding the Qur'ān in terms of philosophical schools of thought. They did not see the Qur'ān as an original source of knowledge, but as a secondary source which would corroborate the knowledge found by their respective philosophical schools. After establishing an idea by their demonstrative arguments, they would look to the Qur'ān to find confirmation from the verses, and if the verses did not confirm their findings, they interpreted them in a way that would comply with what they had rationally concluded.

Like philosophers, the theologians tried to understand the Qur'ān within the framework of their pre-set conceptual boundaries. They similarly tried to understand the communications of God through the filter of their established theological schools. Thus, an Ash'ari would interpret the verses in a way that corroborated their perception of human action as an involuntary occurrence, while a Mu'tazilī would interpret the same verses to mean exactly the opposite. Fayḍ al-Kashani, the author of the classic commentary *al-Safi*, warned people of this type of approach as one of the main barriers to understanding the Qur'ān.

A third way of understanding the Qur'ān, which has been in use for several centuries, and increasingly by contemporary scholars, is through corroboration with scientific theories. When a theory is suggested in scientific circles, the followers of this approach take its truth for granted and look to the Qur'ān for supporting evidence. If the verses are not compatible, they try to reconcile them with their scientific hypothesis. Thus, the Qur'ān is understood in the framework of scientific theories in the same way as the theologians or philosophers tried to understand the Qur'ān using their own dogmas. For instance, in the age of Euclidean astronomy the Qur'ān was a testimony to the truth of Euclid's claim and in the modern age it is a testimony to the Big Bang and Evolution theory.

Finally, some have resorted to a mystical interpretation of the Qur'ān. They purport that there are much deeper meanings under the apparent veil of the words and letters in the Qur'ān. According to them, the Qur'ān has hidden its true meanings under the guise of our spoken language. This method is more problematic than the previous methods. Although there is no doubt that the verses of the Qur'ān have deeper levels and layers of meanings, it is important to first understand the apparent meaning or the *tafsīr* of them. Mystical interpretations are highly subjective and precarious and cannot be regarded as a mode of collective understanding.

Hence, none of these methods are satisfactory or free from a biased understanding of the Book of God. If, in the interpretation of the Qur'ān, the traditions, the philosophical schools, the theological disciplines, the scientific theories, and mystical approaches are not of much benefit due to their subjective and tenuous approaches, then which method should we resort to? How can we understand the meaning of this important communication? The safest technique is the one used by our Imams, peace be on them, and by many exegetes from the early history of *tafsīr*. It is a way of interpreting the verses of the Qur'ān by seeking help from the Book itself. This means finding the meaning of a verse by considering other verses. The Imams did not need such a method, but they used the method to show how the Qur'ān is to be understood, and to demonstrate the safest methodology for understanding the Qur'ān.

This approach is used extensively by Allāmah Tabātabāi in his lengthy commentary of the Qur'ān, *Al-Mīzān*. He believed that the Qur'ān is self-explanatory and does not need anything else to explain it. It is a 'clarification for everything' (16:89), therefore, it cannot need further explanation. The verses which may need interpretation both in terms of terminology and their conceptual meanings could be clarified by other verses. As Amīr al-Mu'minīn, Imam Ali (as) has said in *Nahj al-Balaghah*, sermon 133, 'some parts of it speak with the help of other parts and some pieces testify for other pieces'. Using this method does not preclude knowledge from any other source which may clarify the meaning of a verse further.

In fact, any evidence through which the meaning of a verse may become richer and more accurate is valuable, including: scientific evidence, *hadīth* sources, philosophical or theological argument, or even mystical experiences. One may also seek help from other revealed books, like the Bible, to better understand certain details of stories or historical accounts mentioned in the Qur'ān. This is acceptable so long as the Qur'ān is taken as the benchmark for the authenticity of those materials, as the Qur'ān says itself, 'We have sent down to you the Book with the truth, confirming what was before it of the Book and as a guardian over it' (5: 48). The references must be judged and evaluated by the Qur'ān and not vice versa.

The Qur'ān is a coherent book, and those who believe in it, know that it contains no contradiction. The reader of the Qur'ān can take any sentence of this book to be a proof for another sentence. If in one place, it says something and elsewhere, it apparently contradicts it, we may use these two verses to construct a fuller perspective of what God would have meant in each case. This amounts to looking at the same thing from different perspectives. For example, we may gain an understanding of something from one angle, and a different meaning of the same thing from another angle which may seem contradictory at first, but together they create a multi-dimensional picture and a richer understanding of what God may have intended.

Many stories in the Qur'ān are repeated in this style. By pondering deeply on the various accounts of the same parables, we find that they are not simple repetitions but, in fact, the same stories told from different perspectives to illustrate the full picture of the event. One such example is the most famous story of Prophet Mūsā (a) which is oft-repeated in many chapters of the Holy Qur'ān. One may wonder why God repeats this story again and again in his book, however, on deeper reflection it becomes clear that these are not repetitions but changes of perspective. This type of approach in the text is necessary, especially because the Qur'ān talks about super-natural beings, concepts, and realms, such as, God, the angels, the *'arsh,* the *kursī,* the *lawḥ,* the *qalam*, the Hereafter, Paradise and Hell. These ideas cannot be grasped easily by our conceptual tools. Unless we explore them further, our minds cannot comprehend them.

For this reason, the verses of the Qur'ān regarding one concept or event should be considered in their totality to reveal their true meaning. This is called the *tafsīr* of the Qur'ān by the Qur'ān, and it is the method that I will mainly use in this commentary, insha'Allāh, although I will seek guidance from other sources too, including *ḥadīth*, philosophy, theology and mystical experiences.

Surah Yā Sīn

Names of the Surah

The famous name of this surah is *Yā Sīn* because it begins with these letters. There are, however, other less well-known names for this surah. It is called *Dāfi'ah* (that which repels) because reciting it repels evil and indecency from one's life and character. It is also called *Mu'ammimah* (generaliser) because it brings the good of this life and the next for its reciter in a comprehensive and holistic way.

Based on some accounts, it is the forty-first surah which was revealed in Makkah. In the present order of the Qur'ān, it is surah number thirty-six.

Merits of Recitation

It was well-known amongst the companions of the Holy Prophet (s) that reciting Surah Yā Sīn has great merit and benefit. The Messenger of God told them: 'Yā Sīn is the heart of the Qur'ān, no worshipper would recite it for the sake of God and seeking the Final Abode, unless all their sins are forgiven. So recite it over your deceased ones.'

Reciting Surah Yā Sīn over our deceased ones sends them blessings and spiritual gifts. However, the benefit to the reciter is even greater, because remembering death and our loved ones who have passed away whilst reciting this surah gives the reader a greater appreciation for the higher purpose in life, and sheds light on the reality of human existence in this life as well as in the hereafter. Narrations about the merits of Surah Yā Sīn are extensive, and cannot all be mentioned here. The following is a small collection of those traditions:

Abū Nu'aym reports from the Prophet (s), 'Whoever recites Surah Yā Sīn at night seeking the pleasure of Allāh, he will be forgiven that night.'

Al-Sheikh Al-Ḥurr Al-'Āmili reports in his highly credible book, *Wasā'il al-Shī'a*, from Imam al-Ṣādiq (as), 'Yā Sīn is the heart of the Qur'ān; whoever recites it before going to sleep or during the day before sunset, will be among those who are protected and provided for during their day until night.'

Al-Sheikh Ṭabrasī reports in his *tafsīr*, *Majma' al-Bayān*' from Ubayy ibn Ka'b from the Prophet (s),

> Whoever recites Yā Sīn for the pleasure of God, God forgives them and they will be rewarded the reward of reciting the whole Qur'ān twelve times. If it is recited for a dying person, the

angels would descend on him, ten angels for every letter of it, lining before him and asking forgiveness for him. They witness his departure, take part in his funeral, pray on his body, and will be present in his burial.'

Here is the holy text of the surah.

بِسْمِ اللَّهِ الرَّحْمَٰنِ الرَّحِيمِ

In the Name of Allāh, the All-beneficent, the All-merciful.

يسٓ ﴿1﴾

Yā Sīn!

وَالْقُرْآنِ الْحَكِيمِ ﴿2﴾

By the Wise Qur'ān,

إِنَّكَ لَمِنَ ٱلْمُرْسَلِينَ ﴿3﴾

you are indeed one of the apostles,

عَلَىٰ صِرَاطٍ مُّسْتَقِيمٍ ﴿4﴾

on a straight path.

تَنزِيلَ ٱلْعَزِيزِ ٱلرَّحِيمِ ﴿5﴾

[It is a scripture] sent down gradually from the All-mighty, the All-merciful

لِتُنذِرَ قَوْمًا مَّآ أُنذِرَ ءَابَآؤُهُمْ فَهُمْ غَٰفِلُونَ ﴿6﴾

that you may warn a people whose fathers were not warned, so they are oblivious.

$$\text{لَقَدْ حَقَّ ٱلْقَوْلُ عَلَىٰٓ أَكْثَرِهِمْ فَهُمْ لَا يُؤْمِنُونَ ﴿7﴾}$$

66 | The word has certainly become due against most of them, so they will not have faith.

$$\text{إِنَّا جَعَلْنَا فِىٓ أَعْنَـٰقِهِمْ أَغْلَـٰلًا فَهِىَ إِلَى ٱلْأَذْقَانِ فَهُم مُّقْمَحُونَ ﴿8﴾}$$

73 | Indeed We have put iron collars around their necks, which are up to the chins, so their heads are upturned.

$$\text{وَجَعَلْنَا مِنۢ بَيْنِ أَيْدِيهِمْ سَدًّا وَمِنْ خَلْفِهِمْ سَدًّا فَأَغْشَيْنَـٰهُمْ فَهُمْ لَا يُبْصِرُونَ ﴿9﴾}$$

73 | And We have put a barrier before them and a barrier behind them, then We have blind-folded them, so they do not see.

$$\text{وَسَوَآءٌ عَلَيْهِمْ ءَأَنذَرْتَهُمْ أَمْ لَمْ تُنذِرْهُمْ لَا يُؤْمِنُونَ ﴿10﴾}$$

78 | It is the same to them whether you warn them or do not warn them, they will not have faith.

$$\text{إِنَّمَا تُنذِرُ مَنِ ٱتَّبَعَ ٱلذِّكْرَ وَخَشِىَ ٱلرَّحْمَـٰنَ بِٱلْغَيْبِ فَبَشِّرْهُ بِمَغْفِرَةٍ وَأَجْرٍ كَرِيمٍ ﴿11﴾}$$

79 | You can only warn someone who follows the Reminder and fears the All-beneficent in secret; so give him the good news of forgiveness and a noble reward.

$$\text{إِنَّا نَحْنُ نُحْيِ ٱلْمَوْتَىٰ وَنَكْتُبُ مَا قَدَّمُوا۟ وَءَاثَٰرَهُمْ وَكُلَّ شَىْءٍ أَحْصَيْنَٰهُ فِىٓ إِمَامٍ مُّبِينٍ ﴿12﴾}$$

82 Indeed it is We who revive the dead and write what they have sent ahead and their effects [which they left behind], and We have figured everything in a manifest Imām.

$$\text{وَٱضْرِبْ لَهُم مَّثَلًا أَصْحَٰبَ ٱلْقَرْيَةِ إِذْ جَآءَهَا ٱلْمُرْسَلُونَ ﴿13﴾}$$

94 Cite for them the example of the inhabitants of the town when the apostles came to it.

$$\text{إِذْ أَرْسَلْنَآ إِلَيْهِمُ ٱثْنَيْنِ فَكَذَّبُوهُمَا فَعَزَّزْنَا بِثَالِثٍ فَقَالُوٓا۟ إِنَّآ إِلَيْكُم مُّرْسَلُونَ ﴿14﴾}$$

97 When We sent to them two [apostles], they impugned both of them. Then We reinforced them with a third, and they said, 'We have indeed been sent to you.'

$$\text{قَالُوا۟ مَآ أَنتُمْ إِلَّا بَشَرٌ مِّثْلُنَا وَمَآ أَنزَلَ ٱلرَّحْمَٰنُ مِن شَىْءٍ إِنْ أَنتُمْ إِلَّا تَكْذِبُونَ ﴿15﴾}$$

99 They said, 'You are no other than human beings like us, and the All-beneficent has not sent down anything, and you are only lying.'

﴿ قَالُوا رَبُّنَا يَعْلَمُ إِنَّا إِلَيْكُمْ لَمُرْسَلُونَ ﴿16﴾

103 | They said, 'Our Lord knows that we have indeed been sent to you,

﴿ وَمَا عَلَيْنَا إِلَّا ٱلْبَلَٰغُ ٱلْمُبِينُ ﴿17﴾

103 | and our duty is only to communicate in clear terms.'

﴿ قَالُوٓا إِنَّا تَطَيَّرْنَا بِكُمْ لَئِن لَّمْ تَنتَهُوا۟ لَنَرْجُمَنَّكُمْ وَلَيَمَسَّنَّكُم مِّنَّا عَذَابٌ أَلِيمٌ ﴿18﴾

104 | They said, 'Indeed we take you for a bad omen. If you do not desist we will stone you, and surely a painful punishment will visit you from us.'

﴿ قَالُوا۟ طَـٰٓئِرُكُم مَّعَكُمْ أَئِن ذُكِّرْتُم بَلْ أَنتُمْ قَوْمٌ مُّسْرِفُونَ ﴿19﴾

106 | They said, 'Your bad omens attend you. What! If you are admonished…. Indeed, you are an unrestrained lot.'

﴿ وَجَآءَ مِنْ أَقْصَا ٱلْمَدِينَةِ رَجُلٌ يَسْعَىٰ قَالَ يَـٰقَوْمِ ٱتَّبِعُوا۟ ٱلْمُرْسَلِينَ ﴿20﴾

107 | There came a man hurrying from the city outskirts. He said, 'O my people! Follow the apostles!

ٱتَّبِعُوا مَن لَّا يَسْـَٔلُكُمْ أَجْرًا وَهُم مُّهْتَدُونَ ﴿21﴾

Follow them who do not ask you any reward and they are rightly guided.

وَمَا لِيَ لَآ أَعْبُدُ ٱلَّذِى فَطَرَنِى وَإِلَيْهِ تُرْجَعُونَ ﴿22﴾

Why should I not worship Him who has originated me, and to whom you shall be brought back?

ءَأَتَّخِذُ مِن دُونِهِ ءَالِهَةً إِن يُرِدْنِ ٱلرَّحْمَٰنُ بِضُرٍّ لَّا تُغْنِ عَنِّى شَفَٰعَتُهُمْ شَيْـًٔا وَلَا يُنقِذُونِ ﴿23﴾

Shall I take gods besides Him? If the All-beneficent desired to cause me any distress, their intercession will not avail me in any way, nor will they rescue me.

إِنِّى إِذًا لَّفِى ضَلَٰلٍ مُّبِينٍ ﴿24﴾

Indeed, then I would be in manifest error.

إِنِّى ءَامَنتُ بِرَبِّكُمْ فَٱسْمَعُونِ ﴿25﴾

Indeed I have faith in your Lord, so listen to me.'

قِيلَ ٱدْخُلِ ٱلْجَنَّةَ قَالَ يَٰلَيْتَ قَوْمِى يَعْلَمُونَ ﴿26﴾

He was told, 'Enter Paradise!' He said, 'Alas! Had my people only known

﴿27﴾ بِمَا غَفَرَ لِي رَبِّي وَجَعَلَنِي مِنَ ٱلْمُكْرَمِينَ

124   for what my Lord forgave me and made me one of the honoured ones!'

وَمَآ أَنزَلْنَا عَلَىٰ قَوْمِهِ مِنۢ بَعْدِهِ مِن جُندٍ مِّنَ ٱلسَّمَآءِ وَمَا كُنَّا مُنزِلِينَ ﴿28﴾

128   After him We did not send down on his people a host from the sky, nor We would have sent down.

إِن كَانَتْ إِلَّا صَيْحَةً وَٰحِدَةً فَإِذَا هُمْ خَٰمِدُونَ ﴿29﴾

129   It was but a single Cry, and, behold, they were stilled [like burnt ashes]!

يَٰحَسْرَةً عَلَى ٱلْعِبَادِ مَا يَأْتِيهِم مِّن رَّسُولٍ إِلَّا كَانُوا بِهِ يَسْتَهْزِءُونَ ﴿30﴾

131   How regrettable of the servants! There did not come to them any apostle but that they used to deride him.

أَلَمْ يَرَوْا۟ كَمْ أَهْلَكْنَا قَبْلَهُم مِّنَ ٱلْقُرُونِ أَنَّهُمْ إِلَيْهِمْ لَا يَرْجِعُونَ ﴿31﴾

135   Have they not regarded how many generations We have destroyed before them who will not come back to them?

وَإِن كُلٌّ لَّمَّا جَمِيعٌ لَّدَيْنَا مُحْضَرُونَ ﴿32﴾

137 | And all of them will indeed be presented before Us.

وَءَايَةٌ لَّهُمُ ٱلْأَرْضُ ٱلْمَيْتَةُ أَحْيَيْنَٰهَا وَأَخْرَجْنَا مِنْهَا حَبًّا فَمِنْهُ يَأْكُلُونَ ﴿33﴾

138 | A sign for them is the dead earth, which We revive and bring forth grain out of it, so they eat of it.

وَجَعَلْنَا فِيهَا جَنَّٰتٍ مِّن نَّخِيلٍ وَأَعْنَٰبٍ وَفَجَّرْنَا فِيهَا مِنَ ٱلْعُيُونِ ﴿34﴾

147 | We make in it orchards of date palms and vines, and We cause springs to gush forth in it,

لِيَأْكُلُوا مِن ثَمَرِهِ وَمَا عَمِلَتْهُ أَيْدِيهِمْ أَفَلَا يَشْكُرُونَ ﴿35﴾

149 | so that they may eat of its fruit and what their hands have cultivated. Will they not then give thanks?

سُبْحَٰنَ ٱلَّذِى خَلَقَ ٱلْأَزْوَٰجَ كُلَّهَا مِمَّا تُنۢبِتُ ٱلْأَرْضُ وَمِنْ أَنفُسِهِمْ وَمِمَّا لَا يَعْلَمُونَ ﴿36﴾

154 | Immaculate is He who has created all the kinds of what the earth grows, and of themselves, and of what they do not know.

وَءَايَةٌ لَّهُمُ ٱلَّيْلُ نَسْلَخُ مِنْهُ ٱلنَّهَارَ فَإِذَا هُم مُّظْلِمُونَ ﴿37﴾

156 A sign for them is the night, which We strip of daylight, and, behold, they find themselves in the dark!

وَٱلشَّمْسُ تَجْرِى لِمُسْتَقَرٍّ لَّهَا ذَٰلِكَ تَقْدِيرُ ٱلْعَزِيزِ ٱلْعَلِيمِ ﴿38﴾

160 The sun runs on to its place of rest: That is the ordaining of the All-mighty, the All-knowing.

وَٱلْقَمَرَ قَدَّرْنَٰهُ مَنَازِلَ حَتَّىٰ عَادَ كَٱلْعُرْجُونِ ٱلْقَدِيمِ ﴿39﴾

162 As for the moon, We have ordained its phases, until it becomes like an old palm leaf.

لَا ٱلشَّمْسُ يَنۢبَغِى لَهَآ أَن تُدْرِكَ ٱلْقَمَرَ وَلَا ٱلَّيْلُ سَابِقُ ٱلنَّهَارِ وَكُلٌّ فِى فَلَكٍ يَسْبَحُونَ ﴿40﴾

164 Neither it behooves the sun to overtake the moon, nor may the night outrun the day, and each swims in an orbit.

وَءَايَةٌ لَّهُمْ أَنَّا حَمَلْنَا ذُرِّيَّتَهُمْ فِى ٱلْفُلْكِ ٱلْمَشْحُونِ ﴿41﴾

165 A sign for them is that We carried their progeny in the laden ship,

وَخَلَقْنَا لَهُم مِّن مِّثْلِهِ مَا يَرْكَبُونَ ﴿42﴾

167 | and We have created for them what is similar to it, which they ride.

وَإِن نَّشَأْ نُغْرِقْهُمْ فَلَا صَرِيخَ لَهُمْ وَلَا هُمْ يُنقَذُونَ ﴿43﴾

168 | And if We like We drown them, whereat they have no one to call for help, nor are they rescued

إِلَّا رَحْمَةً مِّنَّا وَمَتَٰعًا إِلَىٰ حِينٍ ﴿44﴾

171 | except by a mercy from Us and for an enjoyment until some time.

وَإِذَا قِيلَ لَهُمُ ٱتَّقُوا مَا بَيْنَ أَيْدِيكُمْ وَمَا خَلْفَكُمْ لَعَلَّكُمْ تُرْحَمُونَ ﴿45﴾

173 | And when they are told, 'Beware of that which is before you and that which is behind you, so that you may receive *His mercy…'

وَمَا تَأْتِيهِم مِّنْ ءَايَةٍ مِّنْ ءَايَٰتِ رَبِّهِمْ إِلَّا كَانُوا عَنْهَا مُعْرِضِينَ ﴿46﴾

178 | There does not come to them any sign from among the signs of their Lord but that they have been disregarding it.

وَإِذَا قِيلَ لَهُمْ أَنفِقُوا مِمَّا رَزَقَكُمُ ٱللَّهُ قَالَ ٱلَّذِينَ كَفَرُوا لِلَّذِينَ ءَامَنُوٓا أَنُطْعِمُ مَن لَّوْ يَشَآءُ ٱللَّهُ

أَطْعَمَهُ إِنْ أَنتُمْ إِلَّا فِي ضَلَٰلٍ مُّبِينٍ ﴿47﴾

179 When they are told, 'Spend out of what Allāh has provided you,' the faithless say to the faithful, 'Shall we feed *someone whom Allāh would feed, if He wished? You are only in manifest error.'

وَيَقُولُونَ مَتَىٰ هَٰذَا ٱلْوَعْدُ إِن كُنتُمْ صَٰدِقِينَ ﴿48﴾

183 And they say, 'When will this promise be fulfilled, should you be truthful?'

مَا يَنظُرُونَ إِلَّا صَيْحَةً وَٰحِدَةً تَأْخُذُهُمْ وَهُمْ يَخِصِّمُونَ ﴿49﴾

188 They do not await but a single Cry that will seize them as they wrangle.

فَلَا يَسْتَطِيعُونَ تَوْصِيَةً وَلَا إِلَىٰ أَهْلِهِمْ يَرْجِعُونَ ﴿50﴾

191 Then they will not be able to make any will, nor will they return to their folks.

وَنُفِخَ فِي ٱلصُّورِ فَإِذَا هُم مِّنَ ٱلْأَجْدَاثِ إِلَىٰ رَبِّهِمْ يَنسِلُونَ ﴿51﴾

192 And when the Trumpet is blown, behold, there they will be, scrambling towards their Lord from their graves!

قَالُوا يَٰوَيْلَنَا مَنۢ بَعَثَنَا مِن مَّرْقَدِنَاۜ هَٰذَا مَا وَعَدَ ٱلرَّحْمَٰنُ وَصَدَقَ ٱلْمُرْسَلُونَ ﴿52﴾

194 They will say, 'Woe to us! Who raised us from our place of sleep?' 'This is what the All-beneficent had promised, and the apostles had spoken the truth!'

إِن كَانَتْ إِلَّا صَيْحَةً وَٰحِدَةً فَإِذَا هُمْ جَمِيعٌ لَّدَيْنَا مُحْضَرُونَ ﴿53﴾

197 It will be but a single Cry, and, behold, they will all be presented before Us!

فَٱلْيَوْمَ لَا تُظْلَمُ نَفْسٌ شَيْـًٔا وَلَا تُجْزَوْنَ إِلَّا مَا كُنتُمْ تَعْمَلُونَ ﴿54﴾

198 'Today no soul will be wronged in the least, nor will you be requited except for what you used to do.'

إِنَّ أَصْحَٰبَ ٱلْجَنَّةِ ٱلْيَوْمَ فِى شُغُلٍ فَٰكِهُونَ ﴿55﴾

203 Indeed today the inhabitants of Paradise rejoice in their engagements

هُمْ وَأَزْوَٰجُهُمْ فِى ظِلَٰلٍ عَلَى ٱلْأَرَآئِكِ مُتَّكِـُٔونَ ﴿56﴾

206 —they and their mates, reclining on couches in the shades.

لَهُمْ فِيهَا فَكِهَةٌ وَلَهُم مَّا يَدَّعُونَ ﴿57﴾

208 There they have fruits, and they have whatever they want.

سَلَـٰمٌ قَوْلاً مِّن رَّبٍّ رَّحِيمٍ ﴿58﴾

211 'Peace!'—a watchword from the all-merciful Lord.

وَٱمْتَـٰزُواْ ٱلْيَوْمَ أَيُّهَا ٱلْمُجْرِمُونَ ﴿59﴾

212 And 'Get apart today, you guilty ones!'

أَلَمْ أَعْهَدْ إِلَيْكُمْ يَـٰبَنِىٓ ءَادَمَ أَن لَّا تَعْبُدُواْ ٱلشَّيْطَـٰنَ إِنَّهُۥ لَكُمْ عَدُوٌّ مُّبِينٌ ﴿60﴾

215 'Did I not exhort you, O children of Adam, saying, "Do not worship Satan. He is indeed your manifest enemy.

وَأَنِ ٱعْبُدُونِى هَـٰذَا صِرَٰطٌ مُّسْتَقِيمٌ ﴿61﴾

229 Worship Me. That is a straight path"

وَلَقَدْ أَضَلَّ مِنكُمْ جِبِلاًّ كَثِيرًا أَفَلَمْ تَكُونُواْ تَعْقِلُونَ ﴿62﴾

230 Certainly, he has led astray many of your generations. Have you not exercised your reason?

هَـٰذِهِۦ جَهَنَّمُ ٱلَّتِى كُنتُمْ تُوعَدُونَ ﴿63﴾

232 This is the Hell you had been promised!

أَصْلَوْهَا ٱلْيَوْمَ بِمَا كُنتُمْ تَكْفُرُونَ ﴿64﴾

238   Enter it today, because of what you used to deny.

ٱلْيَوْمَ نَخْتِمُ عَلَىٰ أَفْوَاهِهِمْ وَتُكَلِّمُنَآ أَيْدِيهِمْ وَتَشْهَدُ أَرْجُلُهُم بِمَا كَانُوا۟ يَكْسِبُونَ ﴿65﴾

239   Today We shall seal their mouths, and their hands shall speak to Us, and their feet shall bear witness concerning what they used to earn.'

وَلَوْ نَشَآءُ لَطَمَسْنَا عَلَىٰٓ أَعْيُنِهِمْ فَٱسْتَبَقُوا۟ ٱلصِّرَٰطَ فَأَنَّىٰ يُبْصِرُونَ ﴿66﴾

245   Had We wished We would have blotted out their eyes: then, were they to advance towards the path, how would have they seen?

وَلَوْ نَشَآءُ لَمَسَخْنَٰهُمْ عَلَىٰ مَكَانَتِهِمْ فَمَا ٱسْتَطَٰعُوا۟ مُضِيًّا وَلَا يَرْجِعُونَ ﴿67﴾

247   And had We wished We would have deformed them in their place; then they would neither have been able to move ahead nor to return.

وَمَن نُّعَمِّرْهُ نُنَكِّسْهُ فِى ٱلْخَلْقِ أَفَلَا يَعْقِلُونَ ﴿68﴾

247   And whomever We give a long life, We cause him to regress in creation. Then, will they not exercise their reason?

وَمَا عَلَّمْنَٰهُ ٱلشِّعْرَ وَمَا يَنۢبَغِى لَهُۥٓ إِنْ هُوَ إِلَّا ذِكْرٌ وَقُرْءَانٌ مُّبِينٌ ﴿69﴾

249 We did not teach him poetry, nor does it behoove him. This is just a reminder and a manifest Qur'ān,

لِّيُنذِرَ مَن كَانَ حَيًّا وَيَحِقَّ ٱلْقَوْلُ عَلَى ٱلْكَٰفِرِينَ ﴿70﴾

251 so that anyone who is alive may be warned, and that the word may come due against the faithless.

أَوَلَمْ يَرَوْا۟ أَنَّا خَلَقْنَا لَهُم مِّمَّا عَمِلَتْ أَيْدِينَآ أَنْعَٰمًا فَهُمْ لَهَا مَٰلِكُونَ ﴿71﴾

253 Have they not seen that We have created for them—of what Our hands have worked—cattle, so they have become their masters?

وَذَلَّلْنَٰهَا لَهُمْ فَمِنْهَا رَكُوبُهُمْ وَمِنْهَا يَأْكُلُونَ ﴿72﴾

255 And We made them tractable for them; so some of them make their mounts and some of them they eat.

وَلَهُمْ فِيهَا مَنَٰفِعُ وَمَشَارِبُ أَفَلَا يَشْكُرُونَ ﴿73﴾

257 There are other benefits for them therein, and drinks. Will they not then give thanks?

وَٱتَّخَذُوا۟ مِن دُونِ ٱللَّهِ ءَالِهَةً لَّعَلَّهُمْ يُنصَرُونَ ﴿74﴾

| 258 | They have taken gods besides Allāh, [hoping] that they might be helped [by the fake deities].

$$\text{لَا يَسْتَطِيعُونَ نَصْرَهُم وَهُم لَهُم جُندٌ مُّحضَرُونَ ﴿75﴾}$$

| 259 | [Yet] they cannot help them, while they [themselves] are ready warriors for them.

$$\text{فَلَا يَحزُنكَ قَولُهُم إِنَّا نَعلَمُ مَا يُسِرُّونَ وَمَا يُعلِنُونَ ﴿76﴾}$$

| 263 | So do not let their remarks grieve you. We indeed know whatever they hide and whatever they disclose.

$$\text{أَوَلَم يَرَ ٱلإِنسَٰنُ أَنَّا خَلَقنَٰهُ مِن نُّطفَةٍ فَإِذَا هُوَ خَصِيمٌ مُّبِينٌ ﴿77﴾}$$

| 265 | Does not man see that We created him from a drop of [seminal] fluid, and, behold, he is an open contender!?

$$\text{وَضَرَبَ لَنَا مَثَلًا وَنَسِيَ خَلقَهُ قَالَ مَن يُحيِي ٱلعِظَٰمَ وَهِيَ رَمِيمٌ ﴿78﴾}$$

| 267 | He draws comparisons for Us, and forgets his own creation. He says, 'Who shall revive the bones when they have decayed?'

قُلْ يُحْيِيهَا ٱلَّذِىٓ أَنشَأَهَآ أَوَّلَ مَرَّةٍ وَهُوَ بِكُلِّ خَلْقٍ عَلِيمٌ ﴿79﴾

268 | Say, 'He will revive them who produced them the first time, and He has knowledge of all creation.

ٱلَّذِى جَعَلَ لَكُم مِّنَ ٱلشَّجَرِ ٱلْأَخْضَرِ نَارًا فَإِذَآ أَنتُم مِّنْهُ تُوقِدُونَ ﴿80﴾

271 | He, who made for you fire out of the green tree, and, behold, you light fire from it!

أَوَلَيْسَ ٱلَّذِى خَلَقَ ٱلسَّمَٰوَٰتِ وَٱلْأَرْضَ بِقَٰدِرٍ عَلَىٰٓ أَن يَخْلُقَ مِثْلَهُم بَلَىٰ وَهُوَ ٱلْخَلَّٰقُ ٱلْعَلِيمُ ﴿81﴾

272 | Is not He who created the heavens and the earth able to create the like of them? Yes indeed! He is the All-creator, the All-knowing.

إِنَّمَآ أَمْرُهُۥٓ إِذَآ أَرَادَ شَيْئًا أَنْ يَقُولَ لَهُۥ كُنْ فَيَكُونُ ﴿82﴾

275 | All His command, when He wills something, is to say to it 'Be,' and it is.

فَسُبْحَٰنَ ٱلَّذِى بِيَدِهِۦ مَلَكُوتُ كُلِّ شَىْءٍ وَإِلَيْهِ تُرْجَعُونَ ﴿83﴾

277 | So immaculate is He in whose hand is the dominion of all things, and to whom you shall be brought back.

COMMENTARY OF THE VERSES

بِسْمِ اللَّهِ الرَّحْمٰنِ الرَّحِيمِ

In the Name of Allah, the All-beneficent, the All-merciful.

All chapters of the Holy Qur'ān, except for Chapter Nine (Surah al-Tauba), begin with the *basmalah*.

On the excellence and importance of the *basmalah* (*Bismi Allāh al-Raḥmān al-Raḥīm*) it is narrated from Imam Ali ibn Mūsā al-Ridha (as) who said, '*Bismi Allāh al-Raḥmān al-Raḥīm* is closer to the Greatest Name of Allah (*al-ism al-aʿẓam*) than the pupil is to the white of the eye.'

Ibn Abbas has narrated from the Prophet (s) that, 'As soon as a teacher tells a child to say *Bismi Allāh al-Raḥmān al-Raḥīm* and the child says it, Allah records immunity (from fire) for the child, his parents and for the teacher.'

Imam al-Ṣādiq (as) is reported to have said: 'No Holy Book ever came down from Heaven except that it began with *Bismi Allāh al-Raḥmān al-Raḥīm*

It is reported from the Prophet (s) that, 'Every work of significance not started with the *bismi Allāh* will remain incomplete.'

Reciting the Book of God is one of the most significant undertakings of those who are in search of divine guidance; and hence if we do not begin this by *Bismi Allāh al-Raḥmān al-Raḥīm*, the goal will remain unaccomplished. Considering this narration, one may wonder how people can accomplish great jobs without even believing in God, let alone mentioning his name. We should bear in mind that efforts which occur and end in this world without having any positive bearing on eternal life (*akhirah*), never have real significance. In other words, matters of this world are incomplete (*abtar*) in their nature.

Throughout history, there have been countless kings who have overthrown other kings, and accomplished their task. But are their actions of enduring significance? They shall not be remembered in any meaningful way by later generations. Rather, their efforts will be the basis of myths and legends. In this world, after a while, everything becomes insignificant except what is done for God. Everything is going to perish except what is done in his direction. 'Everything is perishing except his way.' (28:88)

The revelation of *basmalah* at the beginning of every surah teaches us how we should start reading the revealed guidance by seeking help from the one who revealed it; the one who is merciful to all, and merciful to the guided. Since *basmalah* is a part of every surah, and every surah has its own allocation; its special function and its part and share in the total guince of the Qur'ān; so the *ba'* in *Bismi Allāh* may refer to a different form of help sought from Allah in every chapter. That is why some exegetes have suggested that *Bismi Allāh al-Raḥmān al-Raḥīm* in every surah has a different undertone linked specifically to that surah.

In any case, when we begin reciting the Qur'ān with reliance upon the supreme power of God, we connect to the source of wisdom, which is what we need most to understand the wisdom of the Qur'ān. We start with the name of God and seek help by his name, so that we grasp the intended purpose of this surah.

In discussing the verse, *Bismi Allāh al-Raḥmān al-Raḥīm* two aspects must be explored. The first is its interpretation and meaning, and the second belongs in the field of Qur'ānic Sciences which have significance in interpretation and jurisprudence.

The First Aspect - The Interpretation of Bismi Allāh al-Raḥmān al-Raḥīm

The *bā'* in *Bismi Allāh* is for *isti'ānah*, that is, to seek help. It means I read this surah by seeking help from God; for his guidance and assistance in following what I understand. It may also be for *ibtidā'* that is for beginning. It means I begin reciting in the name of God to seek his blessings in what I recite.

If we take the *bā'* to be for *ibtidā'* then the meaning would be 'I begin my recitation by mentioning the *name* of God.' This is mainly for blessing and to remember Him before proceeding with the recitation. If the *ba'* is for *isti'ānah*, then it means 'I begin my recitation by seeking help from the *name* of God.' In this latter case, the question arises as to why we seek help from the *name* of God and not from God himself. Why *Bismi Allāh* and not *billāh*? The answer is that *ism* used for Allah as *name* is not a word to be uttered. Rather it is an attribute, an act, or a quality that manifests one or more aspects of his eternal essence; and since Allah acts in his creation by those aspects or *names,* it follows that we seek help from them. 'God has the finest names, so appeal to him by those names.' (7:180)

In this sense, depending on the content of every surah, we may seek help from a different name of Allah when we begin our recitation. And this is what some commentators mean when they say the *basmalah* may have a different meaning for every surah.

In the verse *Bismi Allāh al-Raḥmān al-Raḥīm* there are three names of God: *Allāh*, *al-Raḥmān* and *al-Raḥīm*. There is a difference between these three names: Allah is the universal name of God; when we utter this name, we mean God considered with all his infinite names or attributes. It does not refer to any particular name or quality but refers to that supreme being with all his qualities.

However, *al-Raḥmān* and *al-Raḥīm* refer to specific qualities. The root word for both these attributes is *Raḥma*, which means 'mercy'. But the difference in conjugation gives them different meanings. Both conjugates are for hyperbole *'sīghat al-mubālaghah'*, that is to magnify the essence of the quality in the word. They are used to show the extensiveness, the magnitude and the expansion of *raḥma* in God, in multiple ways. Usually, when we use words to magnify the attribute in Arabic, if they have different conjugants and forms, they emphasise that attribute in different ways. In this case, *raḥma* magnifies the quality of mercy in the sense of its generality, extensiveness, and inclusiveness for all. Therefore, *al-Raḥmān*, is someone who dispenses mercy in the most general and the most inclusive way. *Raḥīm*, on the other hand, emphasises the quality of mercy in terms of its continuation, permanence and depth. So, when we call Allah *al-Raḥīm*, it means he has continuous and permanent mercy which permeates into the depth of its subject.

The all-inclusive mercy of God includes everyone and everything. In other words, Allah as *al-Raḥmān* dispenses mercy to all. But the continuous, deep, penetrating mercy is only for those who can receive it. Thus, the ungrateful will be deprived of it because they are unable to accept it. They are deprived of the experience of God in their hearts because they have closed all the doors on him. Imam Ja'far as Ṣādiq (as) has concisely defined these two types of mercy. He said, "*Al-Raḥmān* is a proper noun with a general feature and *al-Raḥīm* is a common noun with a specific feature."

Al-Raḥmān as a descroption, is exclusively restricted to God, but its feature is that it includes everyone and everything. *Al-Raḥīm*, as an adjective can be attributed to God and to people but its feature is that it is restricted in its inclusiveness. In other words, someone who is very merciful could not be called *Raḥmān*; a human being can never be called *Raḥmān*; they can be called *Raḥīm*; *Raḥmān* is used only for Allah. So, Imam Ja'far as Ṣādiq (as) said that this is a special name only for Allah, but it has a general meaning, it means it encompasses everyone and everything. However, *al-*

Raḥīm, is a common name, it is used for human beings and for God in the same sense but it denotes a very particular attribute of God, in the sense that it does not include everyone. Allah is *Raḥmān* towards everything and everyone but not *Raḥīm* towards everyone.

The Holy Qur'ān uses these two terms in the same sense as described by Imam Ja'far as Ṣādiq (as). There are numerous instances in the Qur'ān in which these two terms appear. For example, in Surah Maryam, there is a clear application of the meaning of *al-Raḥmān:*

قُلْ مَن كَانَ فِى الضَّلَالَةِ فَلْيَمْدُدْ لَهُ الرَّحْمَانُ مَدًّا حَتَّىٰ إِذَا رَأَوْاْ مَا يُوعَدُونَ إِمَّا الْعَذَابَ وَ إِمَّا السَّاعَةَ فَسَيَعْلَمُونَ مَنْ هُوَ شَرٌّ مَّكَانًا وَ أَضْعَفُ جُنداً

Say, "Whoever abides in error, the all-beneficent shall prolong his respite until they sight what they have been promised: either punishment, or the Hour." Then they will know whose position is worse, and whose host is weaker. (19:75)

This verse explains that *al-Raḥmān* extends his provision even for those who abide in error. Regarding *al-Raḥīm*, there is a verse in Surah al-Ahzāb, which restricts the mercy of *al-Raḥīm* to the believers.

هُوَ الَّذِى يُصَلِّى عَلَيْكُمْ وَ مَلَئِكَتُهُ لِيُخْرِجَكُمْ مِّنَ الظُّلُمَتِ إِلَى النُّورِ وَ كَانَ بِالْمُؤْمِنِينَ رَحِيما

It is he who blesses you, and so do his angels, that he may bring you out from darkness into light, and he is most merciful to the faithful. (33:43)

This type of *rahma* which is for the faithful has no limit and knows no bounds. The more profound one's faith, the more this mercy penetrates their heart and soul. God talks about some people, saying he admitted them into his special *rahma*. For example, regarding Ishmael, Idris, and Ezekiel, he says: 'we admitted them into our mercy. Indeed, they were among the righteous.' (21:86) Regarding Abraham, Isaac, and Jacob, he says: 'we gave them of our Mercy.' (19:50)

Admission into this type of mercy revolutionises a person completely. Their spiritual eyes are opened due to the reception of that *rahma*. Although whatever we see or hear as ordinary people is facilitated by his help; it is very limited in its extent. When faith increases, the eyes of heart open wider, and in this sense, that *rahma*, would increase and expand.

There is nothing out there preventing us from receiving that special *rahma*, except ourselves. It is still universal, like the *raḥma* which is in *al-Raḥmān*, but it is us who deprive our souls from receiving it. That is why it only embraces the believers. In other words, the restriction is not from God, it is from our side.

These two attributes are mentioned at the beginning of every surah because God wants to inform humankind that whatever they do, even if they are sinful or turn away from him, they are in the folds of the merciful *al-Raḥmān*. It is Allah who provides for everything in the heavens and the earth. If a person wishes to turn to him, he has even more mercy; Allah is *al-Raḥīm*.

The Second Aspect - Is Bismi Allāh al-Raḥmān al-Raḥīm Part of the Surah?

There is disagreement among scholars as to whether *basmalah* (*Bismi Allāh al-Raḥmān al-Raḥīm*) is a part of the surah or just placed there by the Prophet (s) to inform people where one surah ends and another surah begins. This argument belongs to the Qur'ānic Sciences discipline but it has a jurisprudential connotation when it comes to Surah al-Fātiḥah and any surah that we recite in obligatory prayers after al-Fātiḥah. If it is part of Surah al-Fātiḥah then if one does not recite it in *ṣalāt*, their *ṣalāt* would be invalid. By the same token, if it is not part of Surah al-Fātiḥah, then reciting it would make the *ṣalāt* invalid, and the same applies to the surahs recited after al-Fātiḥah in the Shi'a view.

Following Imam Ali (as) the Shi'as have regarded *basmalah* as part of every surah, and especially al-Fātiḥah, to the extent that reciting it loudly in every *ṣalāt* has become a hallmark of Shi'as. '*Al Jahru bi Bismi Allāh al-Raḥmān al-Raḥīm*' is regarded in a *hadīth* to be a sign for every Shi'a believer. This means when they recite Surah al-Fātiḥah and then another surah after it, they are recommended to recite their *Bismi Allāh al-Raḥmān al-Raḥīm* loudly even in noon and afternoon prayers because in their sources it is documented to be the practice of the Prophet (s).

Among the Muslims scholars there are four different views regarding this matter.

1. *Bismi Allāh al-Raḥmān al-Raḥīm* is part of every surah.

2. It is not part of any surah

3. It is part of Surah al-Fātiḥah only

4. It is a verse of the Qur'ān at the beginning of every surah, but is not a part of the surah. That means there are 113 verses of the Qur'ān which are not part of any surah at all.

Among the leading scholars, Imam al-Shāfi'ī and Imam Ahmad Ibn Hanbal believed that *basmalah* is part of the surah. That is why Shāfi'ī and Hanbali

Muslims recite *Bismi Allāh al-Raḥmān al-Raḥīm* in their *ṣalāt*. Of course, there are different opinions within the school about whether it should be recited loudly or quietly. On the other hand, Imam Mālik and Imam Abū Ḥanīfa do not regard *basmalah* as part of any surah. Therefore, Māliki and Hanafi Muslims do not recite it in their *ṣalāt* when they recite Surah al-Fātiḥah. Some Shāfiʿī' scholars, regard it as part of al-Fātiḥah and not part of any other surah so they also recite *basmalah* in their *ṣalāt*. Dāwood al-Dhāhiri, the founder of Dhāhiri school, which no longer exists, and some of the Hanbalis, regard it as an independent verse at the beginning of every surah but not a part of that surah so they too do not recite it when they recite al-Fātiḥah.

The Shi'a scholars unanimously hold that *basmalah* is a part of al-Fātiḥah, and part of every surah, except Surah Tawba, and if anyone intentionally does not say it in his *ṣalāt*, their *ṣalāt* is invalid. Based on narrations of *Ahl al-Bayt* (as), this was the opinion of Imam Ali ibn Abi Tālib (as), which is the most reliable source for *sunnah* of the Prophet (s). In a report Imam Ja'far al-Ṣādiq (as) criticises those who did not regard *basmalah* as part of the Qur'ān by saying, 'What is wrong with them! May God destroy them. They targeted the greatest verse in the Qur'ān.'

Among the Sunni scholars, Ibn Kathir reports in his *tafsīr* that the first four Caliphs used to recite *basmalah* loudly in their *ṣalāt*. However, there are many counter reports that say the Four Caliphs never recited *basmalah* in *ṣalāt*. There are many traditions in confirmation of the first view in Sunni literature. For example, Abū Dāwood and Tirmidhi report that, 'The Prophet (s) used to begin the *ṣalāt* by *Bismi Allāh al-Raḥmān al-Raḥīm*.'

Al-Ḥākim al-Nayshābūri reports in a sound *ḥadīth* that Anas Ibn Mālik said, 'I heard the Prophet (s) reciting the *basmalah* loudly.'

Dāruqutni reports from Ibn Abbas that, 'The Prophet (s) always recited *basmalah* loudly until his soul was taken, may greetings of God be on him.' He also reports from Imam Ali (as) that, 'The Prophet (s) used to recite *basmalah* loudly in both the surahs.'

Finally, Tirmidhi reports from 'Akramah that Ibn Abbas used to begin his *ṣalāt* by *Bismi Allāh al-Raḥmān al-Raḥīm* and used to say that 'it is something that Shaytān has stolen from people'.

It is clear that these narrations in Sunni sources agree with the unanimous view of the Shi'a scholars that *basmalah* is part of the surah and must be recited in *ṣalāt*, although there are counter accounts in Sunni sources which have caused disagreement over the issue.

However, notwithstanding such disagreements, no Sunni scholar would say that mentioning *basmalah* at the opening of *ṣalāt* would invalidate it.

﴿1﴾ يسٓ

Yā Sīn!

'*Yā Sīn*' is one of the disjointed letters of the Qur'ān. It is composed of '*Yā*' and '*Sīn*' which do not have a meaning of their own. The disjointed letters appear at the beginning of 29 surahs and altogether 14 letters are used in them, which constitutes half of the Arabic alphabet. The disjoined letters first appear in Surah al-Baqarah (2), with *Alif, Lām, Mīm* and the last surah in which they appear is the Surah al-Qalam (68), with the letter *nūn* at the beginning. These letters appear in different numbers and different combinations across the Qur'ān. The shortest is only one letter, like *ṣād*, or *qāf* and the longest is composed of five letters like *kāf, hā', yā, 'ayn, ṣād*.

There are more than twenty theories mentioned by exegetes regarding the interpretation of these letters, however, none can provide a conclusive interpretation. Therefore, some have concluded that the disjointed letters fall in the category of the equivocal verses (*mutashābihāt*). However, this is inaccurate since all equivocal verses of the Qur'ān also have an apparent meaning. The equivocal verses are called equivocal because they imply more than one meaning and we do not know which one is the intended meaning. That is why they can be interpreted in different ways and the Qur'ān warns, 'As for those in whose hearts is deviance, they pursue what is equivocal in it, courting temptation and courting its interpretation' (3:7) However, in the case of the disjointed letters there is no apparent meaning at all; they are not words to imply meanings, but they are letters placed beside each other. So, the idea that the disjointed letters are from *mutashābihāt* is not accurate.

Zamakhshari, arguably the greatest Muʿtazilī, exegete, believes that the majority of the commentators of the Qur'ān take these letters to be the names of the surahs in which they appear. So, for example, '*Alif Lām Mīm*' is another name for Surah al-Baqarah or *Nūn* is another name for Surah al-Qalam. There are numerous surahs in the Qur'ān which have more than one name; for example, Surah al-Mu'min is also known as Surah al-Ghāfir, or Surah al-Dahr is also called Surah Insān. In the same manner, Surah al-Baqarah is also called Surah '*Alif Lām Mīm*'. Even in the case of surahs 32 and 41, wherein there is an obligatory *sajdah* in each of them, they name them by the disjointed letters that appear at their beginning. Thus, they call surah 32, '*Alif*

Lām Mīm Sajdah and surah 41, *Ḥā Mīm Sajdah*. This view is adopted by Sheikh Ṭūsi, however, the problem with it is that several surahs would then have the same name. For example, surahs 2, 3, 29, 30, 31, and 32 all begin with *Alif Lām Mīm* and it would mean that six surahs have the same name. Sheikh Ṭūsi would not see any objection in this since the surahs can be distinguished from each other by a second qualifier.

A third common view regarding the disjointed letters is that they are abbreviations for names of Allah. In other words, Allah starts these surahs with his own name but in a condensed form. For example, '*Alif Lām Mīm*' means '*Ana Allāhu aʿalamu* (I am Allah and I know) which is not a combination of names as such, but a sentence describing Allah. They have taken '*Alif*' from the beginning of the first word, '*Lām*' from the middle of the second word and '*mīm*' from the end of the last word. Or, '*Alif Lām Mīm Rā*' means '*Ana Allāhu aʿalamu wa arā* (I am Allah and I know and see). The problem with this view is that the choice of letters from each word is so arbitrary that only someone with inspired knowledge, like the Prophet (s) or an Imam (as), can recognize it.

A fourth opinion, which is related to the above view, is suggested by Saʿīd Ibn Jubayr who was one of the Successors (*Tābiʿūn*) and a great exegete. He believed that by putting the disjointed letters in a particular order we can arrive at the names of Allah. For example, if we put *Alif Lām Rā'* before *Hā Mīm* and put *Nūn* of the Surah al-Qalam after them then we arrive at the name *al-Raḥmān* (ا ل ر ح م ن). Although very creative, the problem with this view is that not all these letters could be arranged together as smoothly as the quoted example. Ibn Jubayr replies to this criticism by saying that it is our lack of knowledge that should be blamed for this, not the actual phenomenon. If we knew how to put all these fourteen letters together, we would end up with *al-ism al-aʿḍam,* the greatest name of Allah.

Following this speculative method, Shi'as and Sunnis have tried to arrange these fourteen letters in such a way as to support their respective creeds. For example, some Shi'as have arranged them as:

- صراط على حق نمسكه (the path of Ali is right we hold to it) or

- على صراط حق نمسكه (Ali is the right path we hold to him).

- On the other hand, some Sunnis have arranged them as كل سني معه صراط حق (with every Sunni there is a right path).

The fifth opinion is that these letters are *qasams* by which God swears an oath to emphasise a point. We know that in many surahs of the Qur'ān, Allah swears by his creation, including: the sun, the moon, the night, the day, the fig, and the olive. In the same manner, these letters have also been used to swear an oath. The problem with this view is that firstly, the preposition of *qasam* is absent in all the cases, and secondly, what is sworn by is unknown to the audience. Usually oaths are taken by things that have some importance or value with the audience with the aim of gaining a sense of authority and acceptance. There would be little impact if an oath is sworn on something incomprehensible.

Another view which is very common among the exegetes of the Qur'ān is that at the beginning of Islam, when the Prophet (s) recited the Qur'ān, the *kuffār* (unbelievers) used to listen, but after they understood what dangers those verses posed to their traditions, they tried to stop people listening to them and created noise and commotion whenever the Prophet (s) started to recite. 'The faithless say, "Do not listen to this Qur'an and hoot it down so that you may prevail."' (41:26) To overcome this stratagem, the style of the surahs changed, and they started to begin by the disjointed letters. This method confused the *kuffār*, because they did not know what these letters meant and they started to listen to see what followed. This view is allegedly based on some rare practice of Arab poets who used to attract the attention of their listeners by shouting a letter at the beginning of their poems. However, what strongly weakens this view is that these letters appear at the beginning of some Madani (surahs revealed in Madinah) like al-Baqarah and Āl-e Imrān where the audience were exclusively Muslims.

None of the above theories can provide a conclusive explanation for the disjointed letters in the Qur'ān. There is another view mentioned by Allāmah Tabātabāi in his famous *Tafsīr al-Mīzān* which is conceptual although inconclusive. He initially concedes that the meaning and the purpose of these letters are unknown to us and they are like codes used between God and his messenger. However, after examining the surahs which begin with these letters he sees a link between every letter used at the beginning of a surah and a set of concepts in that surah.

Therefore, the surahs with common disjointed letters cover shared concepts. For example, every surah starting with *Alif Lām Rā* has a set of concepts related to it and studying the surah and comparing it with other surahs beginning with the same letters would lead to a set of concepts. For example, a surah starting with *Alif Lām Mīm*, would cover a similar set of concepts with other surahs beginning with *Alif Lām Rā*, because some concepts are related to *Alif*, some to *Lām*, some to *Mīm*, and some to *Rā*; and between these two sets of surahs, concepts related to *Alif* and *Lām* must be common. In the same way, Surah al-A'rāf which begins with *Alif Lām Mīm Ṣād* should be comprised of concepts covered in Surah al-Baqarah, for example, and those covered in Surah Ṣād. However, this theory, although appealing, remains mainly conceptual as Allāmah has not explained the details of locating those common concepts.

One final opinion on the subject, which is inspired by Allāmah's theory, is that these letters had great meaning for the Prophet (s) personally, and that they are placed there exclusively for the Prophet (s). Perhaps they are meant to be understood only by the Prophet (s) and not by anyone else; like passwords by which the Prophet (s), and the infallible Imams (as) as his heirs, could enter a totally different sphere of meaning which is not available to others. Thus, when *alif* or *ṣād* or *qāf* was mentioned at the beginning of a surah, in addition to its apparent meanings, the Prophet (s) and the heirs to his knowledge would have found access to a higher realm of meaning with the help of those passwords.

In other words, we recite these surahs without knowing these keywords and we may not fully understand their intended apparent meanings, but those who know the keywords would reach a depth of meaning which is not accessible without the password. This may be the meaning of the *hadīth* reported in *al-Kāfi* which says, 'Only the one who is addressed by the Qur'ān knows the Qur'ān.'

Lastly, on an unrelated point, Yā Sīn is said to be one of the names of the Holy Prophet (s). In his book of *tafsīr*, *al-Tibyān*, Sheikh Tūsi reports a *hadīth* from Imam Ali (as) saying: 'Allah the Exalted has named the Prophet (s) in the Qur'ān with seven names: Muhammad and Aḥmad; Ṭāhā, and Yā Sīn; Muzzammil, and Muddaththir; and Abdullah.'

As per this *hadīth*, Yā Sīn is a name of the Prophet (s), or as mentioned by some an acronym for him meaning, '*Yā Sayyid*' ('O Sayyid') or '*Yā Sāmi' al-Wahy*' ('O Hearer of Revelation'), or according to Ibn Abbas, '*Yā Insān*' ('O Mankind').

وَالْقُرْآنِ الْحَكِيمِ ﴿2﴾

By the Wise Qur'ān,

'By the wise Qur'ān' is an oath (*qasam*) taken by God to emphasise that the next verse: 'You are indeed one of the Messengers,' is true. One might wonder *why* God should take an oath. Usually oaths are required from people who are unreliable; to convince others they are telling the truth. Allah does not need to swear by something to convince us about his truthfulness, and if he did not want to reveal the truth, taking an oath would not alter the situation. In fact, it is not customary for superior authorities to take oaths for what they assert. They only need to declare their assertions and others should follow. So, why should God take an oath at all?

Furthermore, the subject of oaths is usually matters of high importance for both the speaker and the listener. In the case of divine oaths, there is nothing more superior than God who takes the oath. When God is mentioned in oaths, a superior and a sublime concept is invoked. However, when Allah takes an oath, he always invokes something which is inferior to himself. These concepts need to be reconciled.

Two points are worth mentioning here. Firstly, in Arabic language, *qasam* has always been a literary tool used to emphasise importance. It is not only to prove the honesty of the speaker, but to draw attention to the importance of the subject at hand. By making the oath, God is telling us that the subject deserves attention; it deserves to be considered carefully and wholeheartedly. In fact, by taking an oath, the creator lowers himself to our level to tell us about the importance of the concepts he is teaching us. Here God is different to the kings, queens and presidents of this world. They make announcements and expect others to obey, but God explains and relates to us through his kindness, consideration and thoughtful language of the Qur'ān.

Secondly, reflecting on the oaths taken throughout the Qur'ān, we can conclude that their purpose is not to convince the reader about the veracity of the speaker. Rather they are intended to persuade the reader to ponder over the object of the oath itself. In fact, through contemplation the truth of the statement is realised. The object of the oath in this particular verse is the Qur'ān. The oath tells us that through pondering over the Qur'ān and the wisdom contained in it, the reader would come to the true realization; that Muhammad (s) is one of the Messengers.

The Qur'ān is described here as 'wise'. The term used for 'wise' in Arabic is *ḥakīm* which is derived from *ḥikmah*. *Ḥikmah* is that quality in man by which they can distinguish between right and wrong, and good and bad. All good thoughts are based on *ḥikmah* and all acts done rightly are done according to *ḥikmah*. Any person or any book filled with wisdom can be called *ḥakīm*.

Ḥikmah is the knowledge of 'ought', while science and philosophy are the knowledge of 'is'. 'Ought statements' are moral statements, while 'is statements' are declarations of facts. Knowing what 'is' does not necessarily lead us to knowing what we 'ought' to do. That is why the progress of science does not necessarily lead to progress of ethics and morality, and can sometimes result in regressive morals. Humans are given innumerable gifts in their lives: from life itself to power, intelligence, hearing, sight, taste, feelings, wealth, resources and countless more. However, if the wisdom of how to use these gifts correctly and to produce good from them is lacking, they cannot result in happiness. It is only through wisdom that all these gifts turn to blessings. That is why Allah mentions in the Qur'ān that: 'Whoever is granted wisdom, is certainly given an abundant good.' (2:269)

In surah 31, the Qur'ān informs us that Luqman was given wisdom: 'Certainly we gave Luqman wisdom, saying, "Give thanks to Allah."' (31:12) The wisdom was that man ought to thank his creator. Not all of us have that wisdom. Some ask: 'why should we give thanks to him?' 'Does he need it?' 'Does thanksgiving spiritually uplift us?' And many other hidden questions which are disputed among people, all of which prevent us from offering real thanks to him. Only the *wise* know that they ought to offer God unqualified thanks.

The Qur'ān is described as *ḥakīm* because it teaches wisdom and its verses imbue wisdom in whoever seeks it from them. For the wise, it is also a proof of the veracity of the Prophet (s).

$$\text{إِنَّكَ لَمِنَ ٱلْمُرْسَلِينَ ﴿3﴾}$$

you are indeed one of the apostles,

This statement is the reason behind the oath. It is called *jawāb al-qasam* in Arabic. One might question how this oath would convince people to believe in the Prophet (s), as those who did not believe in the Prophet (s) did not believe in the Qur'ān either. So how would swearing an oath by the Qur'ān persuade the disbelievers to admit the Prophet's (s) claim?

The answer goes back to the concept that the wisdom contained in the Qur'ān testifies that it is from a sublime source. That is why the Qur'ān is not described here as glorious (*majīd*), or great (*'adhīm*), or noble (*karīm*), or manifest (*mubīn*). The disbelievers could not see any of these qualities in the Qur'ān. But no wise person could deny the wisdom contained in the book. In other words, the Prophet (s) did not need any miracle other than the Qur'ān to prove that he was a true messenger.

Explaining the verse, 'And if you are in doubt concerning what we have sent down to Our servant, then bring a surah like it, and invoke your helpers besides Allah, should you be truthful' (2:23), some commentators of the Qur'ān have the opinion that the exact meaning of the verse is not that people should 'bring a surah like it' but *'min mithlihi'* means 'bring a surah from someone like him.' It means that such wisdom cannot come from an uneducated person if he is not inspired by a higher source. Even a highly educated person cannot produce such wisdom let alone an unschooled man. However, the Holy Prophet (s) taught and advised Jews and Christians to the extent that some Jewish scholars recognised him. We know that the Bible was translated into Arabic in the second century after Hijrah, hence, even if the Prophet (s) could read Arabic he certainly could not read other languages as he was not formally educated. So, all that information about the past prophets and the past nations, about the law of Moses and the teachings of Jesus testified that he was connected to a higher realm of knowledge. So, 'the wise Qur'ān' is the best proof that 'you are one of the messengers.'

Therefore, if a person wants to find out whether the Prophet (s) was truthful or not they need not search for miracles. Miracles are for a particular time, and can only persuade the people who see them, others who come after them may regard them as legends; or as myths of the past underdeveloped people. The best proof, however, is to go to the Qur'ān and to see for ourselves that this man was a messenger. Thus, this is the reason why 'the wise Qur'ān' is mentioned as an oath here.

$$\text{عَلَىٰ صِرَاطٍ مُّسْتَقِيمٍ ﴿4﴾}$$

on a straight path.

This is the second message that God reveals about the Prophet (s). After 'You are from the Messengers', he says 'You guide on the straight path'. The discussion on 'the straight path' will be detailed in the commentary of verse 61, 'Worship Me. That is a straight path.' Here, we learn that there is a straight path towards God and that Prophet Muhammad (s) is one of those messengers who guide people towards God on that straight path.

This statement has two implications. Firstly, that there is a path through which man can travel towards God and that we are not cut off from our creator, and we can, if we desire, move close to him or to any destination that he has planned for us. The road is open if we have the motivation to travel.

Secondly, the notion of a 'straight' path implies that there are other paths, which are not straight. This is mentioned on several occasions in the Qur'ān. 'Those who prefer the life of this world to the Hereafter, and bar others from the way of Allah, and seek to make it crooked. They are in extreme error.' (14:3) False messengers and distorted religions are examples of a crooked path. Many people may have spiritual feelings or mystical experiences or inner attraction towards a higher being, but they may not be on a straight path towards God. As a result of their spiritual attitude, they attract others to listen to them, and they might seem as if they appeal to the heart, but it may not be the case, as the following verse suggests: 'Among the people is he whose talk about worldly life impresses you, and he holds Allah witness to what is in his heart, though he is the staunchest of enemies.' (2:204)

So, although there may be different paths towards God or towards the destination that God has planned for us, he has intended that the path to him is straight and not contorted in any way. He has presented the straight path and has sent messengers and custodians for that path, 'This indeed is my straight path, so follow it, and do not follow other ways, for they will separate you from his way. This is what he enjoins upon you so that you may be God wary' (6:153).

تَنزِيلَ ٱلْعَزِيزِ ٱلرَّحِيمِ ﴿5﴾

[It is a scripture] sent down gradually from the All-mighty, the All-merciful

---

The English translations usually render *tanzīl* as revelation. However, a more accurate meaning of *tanzīl* is 'sending down gradually'. This emphasises an aspect which may be lost in inaccurate translation. Different terms are used in the Qur'ān to signify revelation, including *wahy, inzāl, tanzīl, ilqā'* and *ta'līm,* each of which looks at the revelation from a different angle.

Descent here is not used in a physical sense, rather it signifies the reduction of the Qur'ān from a high meta-conceptual level to the conceptual level where human faculties can comprehend it. 'This is indeed a noble Qur'an, in a guarded Book, no one touches it except the pure ones, gradually sent down from the Lord of all the worlds.' (56:77-80) The wisdom contained in this Book is not of earthly wisdom, however, it has been reduced for the earthly man to partake of that wisdom. Human beings cannot have access to those meanings in their unreduced form, except those who are aloof and clean from earthly pollutions; not because it is sealed and locked out of reach, but because ordinary humans do not currently have the competence and capacity to touch those meanings.

The Prophet (s) understood those meta-concepts, which no language can explain, but when he wanted to convey it to us, it translates into our language. 'Indeed, we have made it easy by your tongue in order that they may take heed.' (44:58) In other words, the Prophet's soul is like a medium between the sealed book and us; he conveys those meanings to us in terms of the

Qur'ān which is revealed to him by exact wording from God. Those meta-concepts have been revealed to the Prophet (s) on *laylat al-qadr* (*inzāl*) and have been translated for us by God as the Qur'ān in a gradual manner over more than twenty years (*tanzīl*). That is why the Prophet (s) is told 'Do not hasten with the Qur'ān before its revelation is completed for you.' (20:114)

Allah, as the one who sends down revelation refers to himself here as All-mighty (*azīz*) and All-merciful (*raḥīm*). *Azīz* means 'The Mighty'; who is never defeated, nothing can resist his power, nothing is out of his power, and he is not in need of any power. This implies two things, first, Allah has not sent down the revelation because he needs people to believe in him or to obey him. This is why it is followed by the name *al-Raḥīm*. The revelation is sent purely out of his kindness; out of his will to include everyone in the fold of his mercy. Secondly, he would not fail in his mission and the message will find its way to the heart of those willing to receive his mercy 'though the polytheists may be averse.' (61:9)

$$\text{لِتُنذِرَ قَومًا مَّا أُنذِرَ ءَابَاؤُهُم فَهُم غَٰفِلُونَ ﴿6﴾}$$

that you may warn a people whose fathers were not warned, so they are oblivious.

The word *indhār*, to warn, is used frequently in the Qur'ān; in fact, the Prophet (s) is described as *nadhīr* (warner), as well as a *bashīr* (bearer of good news). This warning concerns the consequences of our actions, which manifest in this world and most importantly in the next world. This is the greatest news human beings have ever received from the prophets, and is referred to in Surah al-Naba' as 'the grand news' (78:2). Of course, it is an intuitive knowledge ingrained in the soul and heart, otherwise humankind would not have understood it, but reminders are needed, and this reminder is in the form of a warning. Therefore, this warning is not something that we are completely unaware of; the prophets simply remind us about it, and that is why they are called *mudhakkir* (the one who reminds). All the basic elements of faith are within us and we only need reminders to recollect and refresh ourselves.

The Qur'ān regards the people of Makkah or the contemporaries of the Prophet (s) as 'a people whose fathers were not warned.' This is because the Arab

Prophets like Hūd (a) and Ṣāliḥ (a) who lived several millennia before Islam could not be regarded as warners for the people of Makkah. They lived a long time ago and did not leave any book which could be followed. Moreover, these prophets lived faraway from Hijāz and their people (*qawm*) were different from the people of the Prophet (s). Even though Prophet Ismā'īl (a) had lived in the same area, he lived too long ago to have a connection with the people of Prophet Muhammad (s) and he did not leave a book.

Prophet Mūsā (a) did leave a book and Prophet Isā (a) lived not long before Islam. However, they are not considered as prophets who were to warn all nations including Arabs. Their books were not translated and transmitted to other nations.

The Arabs could not read the Bible; the Bible was only translated into Arabic in the second Islamic century and the Jews who could read that literature would not preach them to the Arabs. That is why, stating their attitude, the Qur'ān says 'They swore by Allah with solemn oaths that if a warner were to come to them they would be better guided than any of the nations. But when a warner came to them it only increased them in aversion' (35:42) and pre-empted their objection so that they would not say, 'The Book was sent down only to two communities before us, and we were indeed unaware of their reading.' (6:156)

There are some people who are mentioned as prophets in narrations and lived very close to the time of Prophet Muhammad (s), for example, Khālid Ibn Sinān and Quss ibn Sā'idah. It is even reported that the Prophet (s) could remember Quss ibn Sā'idah preaching in the 'Ukādh market while the Prophet (s) was still very young. However these personalities were rather callers to the faith of Abraham than claiming to be prophets. They were preachers who may have received some revelation but did not claim any mission. It is reported from Imam Ali (a) that: "Allah appointed Muhammad (s) while no one among the Arabs claimed prophethood or read any divine book."

Hence, it is true to call the period between Prophet Isā (a) and Prophet Muhammad (s), the period of *fatrah* or slumber, because in this period people were 'oblivious' as this verse mentions.

$$\lefteqn{\text{لَقَدْ حَقَّ ٱلْقَوْلُ عَلَىٰ أَكْثَرِهِمْ فَهُمْ لَا يُؤْمِنُونَ ﴿7﴾}}$$

The word has certainly become due against most of them, so they will not have faith.

This statement alludes to one of the principal concepts in the Qur'ān which is mentioned in different chapters with varying expressions. It is understood by Ash'ari commentators as proof of their deterministic viewpoint while other scholars do not have the same conclusion. The basic concept that this verse conveys is that a 'word' has been passed by God in eternity and that 'word' is realized in these people resulting in their disbelief. This 'word' is sometimes expressed in terms of *qawl* as in this verse and sometimes in terms of *kalima* as in:

$$كَذَالِكَ حَقَّتْ كَلِمَتُ رَبِّكَ عَلَى الَّذِينَ فَسَقُواْ أَنَّهُمْ لَا يُؤْمِنُونَ$$

Thus the word of your Lord has been realized against those who transgress that they shall not have faith. (10:33)

Or:

$$إِنَّ الَّذِينَ حَقَّتْ عَلَيْهِمْ كَلِمَتُ رَبِّكَ لَا يُؤْمِنُونَ$$

Indeed, those against whom your Lord's word has been realized will not have faith. (10:96)

These verses tell us that faith and disbelief are not based on mere reasoning and argument. There is a deeper component which has been destined from the eternity. That is why Ash'ari theologians use these verses to argue that when people do not believe, it is because an eternal 'word' is realized in them, not because they have 'chosen' not to believe. This line of explanation is taken by commentators like Ṭabari who takes the verse to mean the punishment has become necessary for most of them because Allah has determined in *Umm al-Kitāb* that they should not believe, and because of this determination they cannot believe and the statement of punishment (*'adhāb*) is necessitated for them.

In a similar line, Al-Qurṭubi explains that the punishment is necessitated for most of them because it has been predestined in the knowledge of God that they are going to die while they are disbelievers. This type of deterministic view is not in agreement with Shi'a and Mu'tazilī line of thinking. According to them, the verse does not talk about predestined faith or disbelief. Rather it states that Allah decreed when he created man, that *if* man acts in certain ways and believes in certain values, he *cannot* believe in God and would meet his punishment. In other words, what is predestined is the universal 'word' that rules over everyone, a word which is realized in certain people due to their voluntary acts. 'Thus the word of your Lord became due against those who transgress that they shall not have faith.' (10:33)

The 'word' or 'statement' which has been passed in eternity and realized in transgressors is a decree which bars the transgressors from believing to the extent that 'it is the same to them whether you warn them or do not warn them, they will not have faith,' (36:10), and 'even though every sign were to come to them, until they sight the painful punishment' (10:97). This is a form of law or procedure which includes anyone who follows a certain course of action. That course of action is explained in Surah Ghāfir (40). This surah narrates the history of people who did not believe and were subject to the eternal *word*:

كَذَّبَت قَبلَهُم قَومُ نوحٍ وَالأَحزابُ مِن بَعدِهِم وَهَمَّت كُلُّ أُمَّةٍ بِرَسولِهِم لِيَأخُذوهُ وَجادَلوا بِالباطِلِ لِيُدحِضوا بِهِ الحَقَّ فَأَخَذتُهُم فَكَيفَ كانَ عِقابِ

وَكَذلِكَ حَقَّت كَلِمَتُ رَبِّكَ عَلَى الَّذينَ كَفَروا أَنَّهُم أَصحابُ النّارِ

The people of Noah denied before them and the [heathen] factions who came after them. Every nation attempted to lay hands on their apostle, and disputed erroneously to refute the truth. Then I seized them; so how was my retribution? That is how the word of your Lord became due concerning the faithless, that they shall be inmates of the Fire. (40:5-6)

Surah Sād (38), mentions a statement by God before Adam and Eve began their life on earth. It reports a conversation between Iblīs and Allah as follows:

When your Lord said to the angels, "Indeed I am about to create a human being out of clay. So, when I have proportioned him and breathed into him of my spirit, then fall down in prostration before him." Thereat, the angels prostrated, all of them together, but not Iblīs; he acted arrogantly and he was one of the faithless. He said, "O Iblīs! What keeps you from prostrating before that which I have created with my own two hands? Are you arrogant, or are you one of the exalted ones?" "I am better than him," he said. "You created me from fire and you created him from clay." He said, "Be gone hence, for you are indeed an outcast, and indeed my curse will be on you till the Day of Retribution." He said, "My Lord! Respite me till the day they will be resurrected." Said he, "You are indeed among the reprieved, until the day of the known time." He said, "By your might, I will surely pervert them all, except your exclusive servants among them." He said, "That is just and I speak justly, I will surely fill Hell with you and all of those who follow you." (38:71-85)

This last sentence is the 'word' which has passed in the primordial time. Whoever follows Shaytān can have no faith and will end up in Hell. Hell is initially created for Shaytān only, but whoever follows him will go to Hell with him. In other words, Hell is not created for us, rather it is us who follow Shaytān to Hell. We are principally created for *Jannah*, but with free will, we can follow Shaytān to Hell.

This eternal statement is explained more clearly in Surah Sajdah (32). 'Had we wished we would have given every soul its guidance, but I passed my just word: "Surely, I will fill Hell with all the [guilty] *jinn* and humans."' (32:13) It means that God has not willed to guide people by force, but they must choose the straight path by their free will. This is because forced guidance does not result in man being placed in the neighbourhood of God in Paradise. But as God has willed to guide by free will, he has justly passed the *word* to drive to Hell those who transgress and act arrogantly. This is fair because when Allah condemned Shaytān to Hell, Shaytān threateningly asked for respite to show God that humans are all arrogant like himself. But God maintained his justice and replied that if they are like you, they will go with you to Hell. This is the meaning of 'the word has certainly become due against most of them.' It is the eternal decree that God had passed over the followers of the Devil.

In Surah Isrā' (17), the justice of this decree is shown in an even clearer expression:

> When we said to the angels, "Prostrate before Adam," they all prostrated, but not Iblīs: he said,

"Shall I prostrate before someone whom you have created from clay?" Said he, "Do you see this one whom you have honoured above me? If you respite me until the Day of Resurrection, I will surely destroy his progeny, all except a few." Said he, "Be gone! Whoever of them follows you, indeed the Hell shall be your requital, an ample reward. (17:61-63)

Having considered the above, 'the word has certainly become due against most of them' would mean that most of them have followed Shaytān. God decreed that they could follow Shaytān by their own free will, that is the statement; and this statement is realized for most of them, that is why they do not believe. So, the statement would not curtail any free will, rather it would reiterate it.

This is expressed in Surah Saba' (34) in a different way. It does not say that the word has been realized in them, but that Shaytān has realized his assumption about them. 'Certainly Iblīs had his assumption come true about them. So, they followed him all except a part of the faithful.' (34:20) Iblīs's assumption was that he would lead humans astray. And of course, his assumption did not come true regarding countless human beings. In fact, anyone who enters Paradise has proven Shaytān wrong in his universal assumption. He expected that only a very few chosen elite could escape him, but there are many who follow those chosen elite (*mukhlaṣūn*) and who end up in Paradise. His assumption comes true only with regards to those who follow him. 'It was decreed upon him that any who followed him, he will mislead him, and guide him to the punishment of Fire.' (22:4)

إِنَّا جَعَلْنَا فِىٓ أَعْنَٰقِهِمْ أَغْلَٰلًا فَهِىَ إِلَى ٱلْأَذْقَانِ فَهُم مُّقْمَحُونَ ﴿8﴾

Indeed We have put iron collars around their necks, which are up to the chins, so their heads are upturned.

وَجَعَلْنَا مِنۢ بَيْنِ أَيْدِيهِمْ سَدًّا وَمِنْ خَلْفِهِمْ سَدًّا فَأَغْشَيْنَٰهُمْ فَهُمْ لَا يُبْصِرُونَ ﴿9﴾

And We have put a barrier before them and a barrier behind them, then We have blind-folded them, so they do not see.

These two verses are a vivid description of the previous verse, 'the word has certainly become due against most of them.' They explain what happens when 'the word' is realized against someone.

Iron collars (*aghlāl*) were fetters that were put on the necks of criminals in which the hands also were tied. Naturally, the collar touched the chin and depending how thick it was it would keep the head up. If it was not thick the chin rested on it and they could see ahead of them, but if it was thick and the chin was pushed up, they could not see.

This is a striking metaphor for the unawareness, ignorance, and confusion of those who do not believe. No matter how hard they try, they cannot see what is around them and they cannot choose the right path. They are also covered from before and from behind. They cannot see the signs of God which so manifestly indicate his existence and his presence. They cannot see the truth in the words of the Prophet (s), nor in the world in which they live, or in the reality of their soul.

Fakhr al-Dīn al-Rāzi has a notable observation here. In his book of *tafsīr*, *Mafātīḥ al-Ghayb*, he says that the hindrances which prevent a person from knowledge of God are either from inside or from outside, and these people are plagued with both. From inside they are fettered and shackled and from outside they are barred and covered. They cannot see the *anfusi* signs, the signs which are within one's soul and being, because their heads are upturned and they cannot see themselves, and they are unable to see the *āfāghi* signs, the signs which are around them, because they are covered from in front and behind.

The covering from the front prevents them from

considering the signs and rational evidence that show the manifest reality of God, and the covering from behind prevents them from going back to their *fiṭrah*, to their innate nature, and seek guidance from there. The verse tells us that in addition to all these hindrances the criminals are also blind-folded. This is the example of a person who lives in utter darkness. His life is darkness upon darkness upon darkness:

> Like the manifold darkness in a deep sea, covered by billow upon billow, overcast by clouds, manifold layers of darkness, one on top of another: when he brings out his hand, he can hardly see it, and one whom Allah has not granted any light has no light. (24:40)

Commentators of the Qur'ān have mentioned different causes for the revelation of these two verses. However, none of them match the context of their revelation, so they are more likely to be an application of the verses rather than the cause of their revelation. The cause of revelation (*sabab al-nuzūl*) is the circumstance in which a verse is revealed. It could be an incident, a question, or a guideline in a situation, which instigates the revelation of a verse or a set of verses. For example, the verses about DhuulQarnayn in Surah Kahf were revealed after a question was posed to the Prophet (s) about him. 'They question you concerning Dhuul Qarnayn. Say, "I will relate to you an account of him.' (18:83) The application of a verse (*jary*), on the other hand, is when a verse is applied to a situation or to answer a question after the verse has already been revealed.

One of the events that commentators have reported can be found in *Majmaʿ al-Bayān* from the *tafsīr* of Abū Ḥamzah al-Thumāli. Abū Ḥamzah reports from Mujāhid from Ibn Abbas that 'once the Quraysh assembled and said when Muhammad enters [*Masjid al-Harām*] we will attack him as one person. The Prophet (s) entered after a while, but Allah 'placed a barrier before them and a barrier behind them' so they did not see him. The Prophet (s) finished his prayer and passed by them while he sprinkled dust on their heads and they could not see him. After the Prophet (s) passed they saw the dust and said Muhammad has bewitched us.'

Although these two verses describe the situation of the unfaithful in a figurative way, some scholars like Allāmah Tabātabāi believe the verses also speak in a metaphorical sense; there are realities that go beyond the allegory. These realities would only become known to us only after we leave this world of matter. Allāmah believes that apart from this life which we apparently see in everyone as well as ourselves, there is another spiritual life for all of us which we are usually unaware of; something which we will only realize after we die. We may be intelligent here, but ignorant in the spiritual dimension; just like we may have sharp vision here, but blind there. These verses may refer to that spiritual dimension of human life in which some are blindfolded, fettered, and covered from before and behind. This is something that we can only see after the veils are lifted: 'You were certainly unaware of this. We have removed your veil from you, and so your sight is acute today.' (50:22)

The spiritual dimension of the people mentioned here is in stark contrast with those who believe and continuously do good. 'Whoever acts righteously, whether male or female, should he be faithful, we shall revive him with a good life.' (17:97) This good life is a life of purity, light and guidance. When a person is revived to that life they see everything differently, and in a new light, with a new explanation, and a different interpretation. With every single atom of this world they feel the presence of God, they see the reason behind the creation, and the reality of themselves and everything around them, depending what level of purity they have attained.

> وَسَوَآءٌ عَلَيْهِمْ ءَأَنذَرْتَهُمْ أَمْ لَمْ تُنذِرْهُمْ لَا يُؤْمِنُونَ ﴿10﴾
>
> It is the same to them whether you warn them or do not warn them, they will not have faith.

This verse answers a critical question about why these people are insensitive towards this important message. The Prophet (s) must have wondered why some people accept the message and receive it with a warm heart, while others reject it. This is the direct consequence of the realization of the *word* in them and the shackles and veils to which they are subjected. Those who do not respond to the warning have lost all sensitivity towards guidance. The verse also demonstrates that the journey away from God is lengthy and becoming desensitised to his signs and the spiritual message takes a long time. The spiritual seals, veils and fetters are gradual. In their original nature, human beings should be sensitive to the message of God.

In Surah Fussilat (41), God refers to an interesting conversation between the Prophet (s) and the disbelievers. Here, the disbelievers try to use this concept as a counter-claim against the Prophet (s):

They say, "Our hearts are in veils from what you invite us to, and there is a deafness in our ears, and there is a curtain between us and you. So, act [as your faith requires]; we too are acting [per our own]. (41:5)

This is exactly how Allah describes the disbelievers in Surah Yā Sīn. The retort here is very obliging, and focuses on the commonalities between the Prophet (s) and unbelievers: 'Say: "I am no more than a human being like you, who is being inspired that your God is one God, therefore you shall be upright towards him and ask his forgiveness."' (41:6) In his humanity the Prophet (s) can relate to all those around him, but if others are insensitive or lack sympathy, it is what they have brought on themselves.

إِنَّمَا تُنذِرُ مَنِ ٱتَّبَعَ ٱلذِّكْرَ وَخَشِيَ ٱلرَّحْمَٰنَ بِٱلْغَيْبِ فَبَشِّرْهُ بِمَغْفِرَةٍ وَأَجْرٍ كَرِيمٍ ﴿11﴾

You can only warn someone who follows the Reminder and fears the All-beneficent in secret; so give him the good news of forgiveness and a noble reward.

Although the Prophet (s) is a warner, not everyone benefits from his warnings. As mentioned in previous verses, for some there is no difference whether or not they are warned. The warning affects only those who have two qualities; they follow the Reminder (*dhikr*) and fear the All-Beneficent in secret (*ghayb*).

Most of the exegetes believe that the Reminder (*dhikr*) refers to the Qur'ān, because the Prophet (s) reminds people with the Qur'ān. So, the warning only avails those who connect with the Qur'ān and desire to follow it. Those who are indifferent towards it would not be affected.

The second quality is fear of the creator. Although *al-Raḥmān* means the All-Beneficent, it can also refer to the creator, because his universal beneficence manifests itself in his creation. To believe in the creator is intuitive and a prerequisite for accepting any warning. This intuitive knowledge about the creator leads the believer to a sense of fear even though he is absent and unseen. They ask: do I have any duty towards him, how should I thank him, what is his purpose in creating me? Unless there is such a prior fear or concern in a person's heart and soul, they would not seek guidance and would not be reminded by the warning. That is why the Prophet (s) 'can only warn those who follow the Reminder and fear the All-beneficent in secret.'

The adverb 'in secret' (*bi al-ghayb*) has been understood in different ways. The most common understanding is as mentioned above; fear of the creator while he is unseen. However, some have taken it to mean they fear him in secret in their hearts, or in private as opposed to in public, or while they have not seen the *akhirah*. Fakhr al-Dīn al-Rāzi believes that following the Reminder refers to faith while fearing the All-Beneficent refers to righteous acts (*al-'amal al-ṣāliḥ*). That is why it is followed by the good news of forgiveness and a noble reward. They receive forgiveness (*maghfirah*) because of their faith, and are rewarded the noble reward for their good deeds.

The Prophet (s) gives good news (*tabshīr*) at the same time as he warns (*indhār*), as one is the counter side of the other. The good news he brings is the knowledge that life does not simply end with death as the final station of our journey; we shall be granted eternal life. Those who fear the Creator and follow the Reminder will eventually enter Paradise, despite their shortcomings, mistakes, and sins, for there is the promise of divine forgiveness. Thus, upon entering Paradise, they will receive a noble reward.

> إِنَّا نَحْنُ نُحْيِ ٱلْمَوْتَىٰ وَنَكْتُبُ مَا قَدَّمُوا۟ وَءَاثَـٰرَهُمْ وَكُلَّ شَىْءٍ أَحْصَيْنَـٰهُ فِىٓ إِمَامٍ مُّبِينٍ ﴿12﴾
>
> Indeed it is We who revive the dead and write what they have sent ahead and their effects [which they left behind], and We have figured everything in a manifest Imām.

Indeed, it is we who revive the dead; Allah is close while he is far away; he is closer to us than our jugular vein, but at the same time he is sublime and inconceivable so that no contemplation can ever reach him. We read in dua al-Jawshan al-Kabīr:

> يَا مَنْ دَنَا فِى عُلُوِّهِ يَا مَنْ عَلَا فِى دُنُوِّهِ
>
> O he who is near in his majesty and is majestic in his nearness.

When Allah wants to emphasise his nearness to us he usually refers to himself as 'I', and when he wants to signify his exalted and illustrious position he usually refers to himself with the majestic 'we'. Here because reviving the dead necessitates that grand position, the majestic 'we' is used. It is highlighted by the emphatic preposition *inna* which means 'indeed we' and is corroborated by another 'we' (*naḥnu*) to signify that only he is able to do this.

Reviving the dead is not more difficult than giving life in the first place. Although difficulty and ease have no meaning for God, the Qur'ān mentions, based on our understanding, that 'It is he who originates the creation, and then he will bring it back and that is more simple for him.' (30:27) Actions become difficult when there is a limitation in power, resources or intelligence – these limitations do not apply to God. That is why the verse emphasises 'it is we who revive the dead' to explain how this extraordinary phenomenon is made possible.

And write what they have sent ahead and their effects [which they left behind]. This indicates that it is not a simple revival. Rather the revival entails the preservation of whatever a soul has earned in this life. Here, writing and recording actions are not done in order to remember what is otherwise forgotten. God has all-encompassing knowledge of everything. Rather, it involves the preservation of whatever has taken place in life. This act of preservation is done by certain angels who are created for this purpose. They can preserve, in themselves, what a person does with all layers of their intentions, attitudes, and backgrounds.

Every act has countless dimensions that are unknown to us. We may bow down in *ṣalāt* or recite a verse of the Qur'ān; behind that bowing or speech, there are purposes, intentions, hopes, fears, sincerities or insincerities. We may quote a verse of the Qur'ān to harm someone or to guide them; to fulfil a selfish desire; or to remember God. Actions are affected by a person's gender, background, attitude, culture and complexity. In every action, there are so many hidden aspects involved which are difficult to discern. To capture all these, a very complicated recorder is needed; these are the recording angels. They preserve the records in a way that allows them to manifest in distinct ways at every stage and dimension. On Resurrection Day the records of actions manifest in a different way to how they appear in *barzakh,* or how they appear in this world. 'Indeed our messengers write down what you scheme.' (10:21) 'He says no word but that there is a ready observer beside him.' (50:18)

There are *hadīths* that mention two angels who record our earnings; one for the good deeds, and one for the bad deeds. The concepts of writing, book, and pen are very different here. This record is not written with a pen and paper, rather, the angels are the books themselves, or they create an existential preserved entity which is called our book.

One interesting point is that the nature of our good deeds and bad deeds are so different that they cannot be preserved in one place. Therefore, it is not possible for one angel to preserve everything; it is necessary to have different mediums for different types of actions.

This is why there is one angel for writing good deeds, and another for writing bad deeds. In that realm, good and bad cannot exist side by side and they must be distinguished and separated from each other.

After we die and our impact comes to an end, the book of deeds is closed and preserved and the angels are relieved of their duty. Our record of actions is preserved in a greater book, or greater angel, and the separation of good and bad continues to be observed.

> No indeed! The book of the vicious is indeed in *Sijjīn*; and what will show you what is *Sijjīn*? It is a written book. Woe to the deniers on that day. (83:7-10)

> And: The book of the pious is indeed in *Illīyūn*. And what will show you what is *Illīyūn*? It is a written book, witnessed by those brought near [to Allah]. (83:18-21)

These books are stored there until the Day of Judgement when they unfold and manifest what is inside them to their owners. 'We shall bring it out for him on the Day of Resurrection as a wide-open book that he will encounter. Read your book! Today your soul suffices as your own reckoner.' (17:13-14) Interestingly, these books are kept there while they are attached to their owners at the same time.

It is important to mention here that this system is coherent only if we have free will and do things with our own choice. But we know that in many cases, although people have free will, their choices are affected by factors outside their control. Sometime we do things under the pressure of circumstances which impose themselves so strongly that our free will is overwhelmed. So will Allah judge us according to our free will, or according to those circumstances?

This question is answered in Surah Mu'minūn, 'we task no soul except according to its capacity, and with us is a book that speaks the truth, and they will not be wronged.' (23:62) That book speaks the all-encompassing truth about every person; their family, culture, religion, gender, birthplace, circumstances, their wealth, education and many other factors. All these circumstances are taken into consideration and a judgement is passed based on them. Amazingly, the judgement will be passed in such a way that everyone will concede and admit that it is just.

And their effects [which they left behind]; It is not only our actions that are recorded, but what we leave behind as well, our *āthār*. Two meanings have been suggested by the exegetes regarding this statement depending on how they understand the term. *Āthār* is the plural of *athar* which literally means footstep and from there a trace, an effect, or something left behind.

Those who have taken *athar* to mean footstep, have related this verse to a specific case reported from the time of the Prophet (s). Some of the Anṣār from the tribe of Banu Salama who lived in the suburbs of Madinah complained of their remoteness from the Prophet's (s) mosque. This verse was revealed telling them that every step they take towards the mosque is recorded for them as a good deed. In some versions of the *hadīth*, they were intending to move closer to the mosque but the Prophet (s) told them:

إن الله يكتب خطواتكم و يثيبكم عليه فالزموا بيوتكم

Allah writes your footsteps and rewards you for it, so stay where you are.

This version has triggered a jurisprudential discussion among different schools of Sunni *fiqh* as to which is better; living nearer to the mosque or living farther away from it. However, this interpretation does not conform with the context of the verses, and if such a conversation has taken place between the Prophet (s) and Banu Salama, it means that the Prophet (s) has cited this verse which was revealed in Makkah as a confirmation of the reward for their travel to the mosque in Madinah.

A more satisfactory interpretation is to take *āthār* to

mean the effects which are left behind. Therefore, what is sent forward, as well as what is left behind in terms of actions, are both written. When we leave this world, we leave behind property, wealth, children, established charities, knowledge, and whatever good or bad we have institutionalised in our lifetime, which may have continued to have a positive or negative impact for some time. These impacts are included in the record of our actions as long as they continue. They become part of our living history although we are not alive when they take effect. This is the meaning of the statement reported from the Prophet (s) that:

> Whoever institutes a good custom for him is its reward and the reward of those who follow it while nothing is reduced from the reward of the followers; and whoever institutes a bad custom for him is its burden and the burden of whoever follows it.

A charitable offspring, a book which may guide or misguide generations, an institution which may benefit or harm generations are instances of our impacts after our death. In other words, the book of our actions is not closed at the time of our death. If someone leads a group of people astray, and after several thousands of years, people are still led astray because of that person, it is all written for him as well.

Another *hadīth* from the Prophet (s) says: 'When the son of Adam dies, his actions stop except in three things; a running charity, or knowledge from which people benefit, or an upright child who prays for him.' If this is true, we can imagine, for instance, that, whatever 'good' a Muslim accomplishes in their faith is, in a sense, the impact of the Prophet's (s) life after his death.

So, if someone builds a mosque and people come and pray in that mosque until the Day of Judgement, the impact of his act will be written for him. If someone sets up a foundation and people benefit from that foundation after his death, then that is going to be recorded for him. In fact, every single person benefitting from that act is a new kind of action written for the founder.

On the negative side, this does not contradict with the verse in Surah Najm, 'no bearer shall bear another's burden' (53:38), because nothing is reduced from the burden of the followers; the initiators are not going to take those burdens; rather they are going to take extra burdens, which are in fact a repercussion of their own actions, as it is stated in Surah 'Ankabūt:

> The faithless say to the faithful: "Follow our path and we will carry your sins." But they cannot carry anything from their sins, they are indeed

liars! They will carry their own burdens as well as burdens with their burdens, and they will be asked on the day of resurrection regarding what they used to fabricate. (29:12-13)

And we have figured everything in a manifest Imām; The previous discussion related to the book of action of every individual. The concluding sentence of the verse talks about something grander; a book which contains everything: the Book of Creation. This is one of the most fascinating, mesmerising yet bewildering and complicated concepts mentioned in the Qur'ān. All exegetes agree that a 'manifest *Imām*' here means a manifest book, however, considering the meaning of *imām*, it should be a book that leads, such as a book of instructions which leads and guides. That is why the Tawrāt is also called an *imām*. 'And before this [we sent] the Book of Moses as an Imam and a mercy.' (46:12) The Tawrāt was an *imām*, because it guided people. It went ahead of the people and they followed it. So, every book which leads and is followed could be called an *imām*.

The issue here is that this 'manifest *imām*' is the Book of Creation rather than the record of actions, because God states that everything is figured in this book, and since it is an *imām*, it means that the creation must follow the pattern determined in this book. Therefore, this book is not written as a record, after things happen, rather it is written *before* things take place. Before a thing comes into creation, it is written in this book. This is the book from which the angels read their instructions. It is their *imām*. However, this does not negate the conception of gradual creation and free will. In fact, without this book, creation would be in chaos. It is the pattern that life follows. It is similar to our DNA, which is the book that our biological development follows, containing our every physical aspect, from the colour of our eyes to features of our brain.

Every species has a book of their own, human beings follow a pattern which is written in their genes, monkeys and birds follow other patterns. Monkey's genes do not produce birds or vice versa. Above that, every individual creature has a unique book for themselves. God is the creator of these patterns and many more: a pattern before the physical world, in the metaphysical world from which creation follows – this is *imāmun mubīn* (the manifest book). God is the creator of these patterns and many more. Now, apart from these individual books or patterns, there is a Grand Book after which the whole creation is modeled and developed. That is imāmun mubīn (the manifest book). It is the DNA of the whole creation.

In his commentary on this verse, Sheikh Tūsi succinctly alludes to two very important concepts.

Firstly, he says that the Manifest Book is the Protected Tablet (*al-Lawḥ al-Maḥfūz*) and the reason for figuring everything there is so that the angels can read from it and know what should come into being. Secondly, this verse indicates the detailed knowledge of God regarding the creation. Here, he is refuting the view of some of the philosophers of his time who believed that knowledge of God does not include knowledge of the details of matters, rather it is only an overall knowledge of creation.

Everything regarding the creation is already figured in a book which sets the pattern of creation. Fascinatingly, the Qur'ān tells us that this also includes events that will happen in the future. 'No affliction visits the earth or yourselves but it is in a Book before we bring it about; that is indeed easy for Allah.' (57:22) One might question whether this contradicts our free will. The idea that we can sometimes stop things from happening, or cause things to happen needs to be reconciled with the idea of a book having figured everything before it happens.

The Qur'ān tells us that before things happen in this world, there is another world, another dimension, in which these things are created, somewhere before this world, not in terms of time, but in terms of rank and strength. Everything in this world follows the pattern set in that realm. For God, who is outside time, the present, past or future have no meaning. So, whatever people are going to do in one-thousand years is already clearly written in that book. They do it with their own free will but the one who sits outside time has already figured what we are going to do with our own free will and has compiled it in a manifest *imām*:

> With him are the treasures of the Unseen; no one knows them except him. He knows whatever there is in land and sea. No leaf falls without his knowing it, nor is there a grain in the darkness of the earth, nor anything fresh or withered but it is in a manifest Book. (6:59)

And:

> You do not engage in any work, neither do you recite any part of the Qur'an, nor do you perform any deed without our being witness over you when you are engaged therein. Not an atom's weight escapes your Lord in the earth or in the sky, nor is there anything smaller than that, nor bigger, but it is in a manifest Book. (10:61)

Therefore, whatever is going to happen is already witnessed and compiled somewhere which is not in this world. For him all of time exists all at once, but we are standing on different points of that time spectrum.

When we say that we are created on the pattern of our chromosomes, it means that the chromosomes are our point of reference. They are the reference according to which all our cells are created. In Arabic, this reference is called *umm;* mother is called *umm* because children refer to their mothers all the time. Accordingly, the *Manifest Book* is also called *umm al-kitāb* ('the Book of Reference'). So *imāmun mubīn*, *kitābun mubīn* and *ummu al-kitāb* do not refer to different things; they are all one thing from different perspectives.

In conclusion, this verse demonstrates that everything in this world is organized, systematic, and works according to a precise plan. Nothing happens haphazardly, by chance, or by accident; everything is measured, 'Indeed we have created everything in a measure.' (54:49) This does not contradict our free will because our choices are also calculated and incorporated in that Book by God for whom the present, the past, and the future are the same.

وَٱضْرِبْ لَهُم مَّثَلًا أَصْحَٰبَ ٱلْقَرْيَةِ إِذْ جَآءَهَا ٱلْمُرْسَلُونَ ﴿13﴾

Cite for them the example of the inhabitants of the town when the apostles came to it.

An example is put forward for people who rejected the Prophet (s) in Makkah and in later generations. This is the example of a city, which rejected the messengers, the *mursalūn*.

Cite for them the example; The Arabic term used here for 'example' is *mathal*. *Mathal* is used in the Qur'ān in four different ways. The first way, which is used in this verse, is a true event or story of people, cited to convey a lesson or a concept to the reader. The second sense is a parable, where a hypothetical story is mentioned to illustrate a concept. 'Allah draws a *mathal*: a man jointly owned by several contending masters, and a man belonging entirely to one man: are the two equal in comparison' (39:29). The third sense in which *mathal* is used is for simile:

> Cite for them the *mathal* of the life of this world, like the water we send down from the sky. Then the earth's vegetation mingles with it. Then it becomes chaff, scattered by the wind. And Allah is omnipotent over all things. (18:45)

All three ways of *mathal* - example, parable, and simile - are used to illustrate concepts that usually require deeper contemplation.

The forth meaning of *mathal* used in the Qur'ān means 'description'. 'His is the loftiest description (*mathal*) in the heavens and the earth. And he is the All-mighty, the All-wise' (30:27); and 'For those who do not believe in the Hereafter there is an evil description (*mathal*), and the loftiest description (*mathal*) belongs to Allah, and he is the All-mighty, the All-wise.' (16:60)

Of the inhabitants of the city; The Arabic term used here for town is *qaryah*. *Qaryah* originally means a place where people gather to live; and sometimes the people themselves are called *qaryah* or *qarn*. Therefore, it has a broad meaning that can include villages, towns, cities and even civilizations.

This verse and the following few verses cite the true story of a city that rejected the messengers. Most of the exegetes believe that the city was Antioch. Antioch was a flourishing city of ancient Rome in Syria. Its ruins now lie near the modern city of Antakya, in southern Turkey. However, there is a disagreement about whether these messengers were prophets sent by God or disciples of Prophet Isā (a) sent to Antioch by him. A couple of narrations have also been mentioned in both Sunni and Shi'a books elaborating on the story. However, they do not match the description given by the Qur'ān.

The history does not record Antioch's destruction after Prophet Isā (a); furthermore, Antioch was the first city which became a Christian stronghold and its people responded positively to the disciples. So, if this is about Antioch, it must have happened before the time of Prophet 'Isā (a) and if it is related to the disciples it must be another city.

When the apostles came to it; Whether these messengers came one after another, or they all came together, is clarified by the following verse.

إِذْ أَرْسَلْنَآ إِلَيْهِمُ ٱثْنَيْنِ فَكَذَّبُوهُمَا فَعَزَّزْنَا بِثَالِثٍ فَقَالُوٓا إِنَّآ إِلَيْكُم مُّرْسَلُونَ ﴿14﴾

When We sent to them two [apostles], they impugned both of them. Then We reinforced them with a third, and they said, 'We have indeed been sent to you.'

When we sent to them two [apostles]; Those who believe these messengers were sent by Prophet Isā (a) usually claim that first he sent two of the disciples but they were imprisoned by the king; then he sent Sham'ūn (Simon Peter) in their support. The narrations say that Sham'ūn managed to convince the king to release the two disciples. However, this story is contrary to what the verses say and we have no choice but to discard these narrations in explanation of these verses.

This verse shows that it is possible that multiple messengers can be sent to people at the same time.

Sometimes one man cannot accomplish the mission alone. A prime example is the case of Prophet Mūsā and Harun (a) who were sent together. The Qur'ān mentions the request of Prophet Mūsā (a) upon his appointment to the mission as follows;

> Appoint for me a minister from my family, Aaron, my brother. Strengthen my back through him, and make him my associate in my affair. (20:29-32)

Or:

> Aaron, my brother he is more eloquent than me in speech. So send him with me as a helper to confirm me, for I fear that they will impugn me. (28:34)

Aaron was 'more eloquent in speech' in Hebrew, because Musa (a) was raised among the Egyptians and could not speak Hebrew as well as Aaron.

At any rate, some narrations indicate that at times more than seventy prophets were preaching among Banū Isrā'īl at the same time.

Then we reinforced them with a third; The third messenger would have been someone of status and acceptability either among the people or with the king, otherwise sending him would not have supported the cause.

$$\text{قَالُوا مَا أَنتُمْ إِلَّا بَشَرٌ مِّثْلُنَا وَمَا أَنزَلَ ٱلرَّحْمَٰنُ مِن شَىْءٍ إِنْ أَنتُمْ إِلَّا تَكْذِبُونَ ﴿15﴾}$$

They said, 'You are no other than human beings like us, and the All-beneficent has not sent down anything, and you are only lying.'

They said; Here, 'they said,' refers to the authorities who were representing the people. It is also possible that only the powerful authorities opposed the prophets and silenced the majority. The prophets usually began their invitation to God's message by speaking to common people, but this often resulted in a trial in courts or palaces because they were regarded as a threat. Cases like the story of Prophet Mūsā (a) who directly went to the court of Firawn are exceptions.

Therefore, these arguments are usually between a prophet and a king or someone in authority, however, since these positions are trivial for Allah, he mentions them as ordinary people. One example of this matter is the conversation between Prophet Ibrahim (a) and the powerful Nimrud:

> Have you not considered him who argued with Abraham about his Lord, because Allah had given him kingdom? When Abraham said, "My Lord is he who gives life and brings death,"

he replied, "I too give life and bring death." Abraham said, "Indeed Allah brings the sun from the east; now you bring it from the west." The faithless one was dumbfounded. And Allah does not guide the wrongdoing lot. (2:258)

Notice how Nimrud is mentioned with such a pejorative term.

You are nothing but humans like us, and the All-beneficent has not sent down anything, and you are only lying; They thought that because the prophets were human, they must be lying as the All-beneficent cannot send revelation to human beings.

There are two points worth contemplating in this verse. Firstly, they believed in the All-beneficent - this is another term for God or the creator. Mostly all idolaters believed in a creator who had created both the universe and their demigods. The only difference was that they worshipped the demigods rather than the creator, because they thought their fortune and misfortune was decided by the demigods and not the creator. The Qur'ān clearly mentions this with regard to the Arab idolaters. 'If you ask them, "Who created the heavens and the earth?" they will surely say, "Allah."' (39:38)

Secondly, they thought that if the All-beneficent

wanted to communicate with man, he would do it through angels rather than human beings. One of their most significant pretexts for rejecting the prophets was they were humans like us. This is reiterated in many verses of the Qur'ān. 'Nothing kept the people from believing when guidance came to them, but their saying, "Has Allah sent a human as an apostle?"' (17:94), or

> Has there not come to you the account of those who were faithless before? They tasted the evil consequences of their conduct, and there is a painful punishment for them. That was because their apostles used to bring them manifest proofs, but they said, "Shall humans be our guides?!" So, they disbelieved and turned away. (64:5-6)

It means they could not accept that a human being could receive a message from God.

This misconception is sometimes found among the believers but from a different angle. They feel that the prophets are more than human beings because an ordinary human cannot receive communication from God. The difference between the two is that one group say they are not ordinary human beings, and they receive revelation and we accept them, and the other group say they are human beings so they do not receive revelation. This misconception is very common and prevailing among all humanity in all ages. But God refutes this, saying, 'Had there been angels in the earth, walking around and residing [in it like humans do], we would have sent down to them from the heaven an angel as apostle.' (17:95)

In fact, many views from the polytheists are derived from the notion that people who have a deep connection with God, cannot be human beings, and that human beings are not capable of receiving revelation. They are either gods, or God incarnates, or angel incarnates or God himself in the form of the human beings. But God asks, 'Does it seem odd to the people that we have revealed to a man from among themselves?' (10:2) Why should it seem odd? This is the result of misconceptions about God and about human beings. 'They do not value God the way he should be valued when they say: "God has not sent down anything to a human being."' (6:91)

And you are only lying; The accusation of lying against the prophets has been prevalent throughout history despite all the miracles they showed to their unwelcoming audience. This was despite the fact that the prophets were usually known amongst their people for honesty and integrity.

$$\text{قَالُوا رَبُّنَا يَعْلَمُ إِنَّا إِلَيْكُمْ لَمُرْسَلُونَ ﴿16﴾}$$

They said, 'Our Lord knows that we have indeed been sent to you,

This is the conclusion of their discussion after all other arguments have failed. This is in keeping with the style of the Qur'ān; it skips time, it skips places, it skips arguments, and only mentions the crucial parts of every event or story. Here we have to understand that these short sentences were not all they exchanged with each other. Rather they are the highlight of many arguments at the end of which the messengers said, God 'knows that we have indeed been sent to you', and your fate will be in his hands. As Sheikh Tūsi remarks, this sentence is a strong warning to them.

$$\text{وَمَا عَلَيْنَا إِلَّا ٱلْبَلَٰغُ ٱلْمُبِينُ ﴿17﴾}$$

and our duty is only to communicate in clear terms.'

Two matters are clarified by this statement. Firstly, the prophets are only conveyers of the message and cannot force anyone to believe. Having faith is a personal choice that every individual should make for themselves after hearing the message. This is clearly stated in 'There is no compulsion in religion: rectitude has become distinct from error.' (2:256) Secondly, the delivery of the message must be clear and well-defined before any judgment is passed about the people. This clarity is expected in three areas. First, the character of the messenger should be reliable so that people know their honesty, righteousness, and integrity. Second, the message must be consistent, rational, and penetrating. And third, all these should be corroborated by a miracle. Allah has given these three aspects to all his messengers.

قَالُوا إِنَّا تَطَيَّرْنَا بِكُمْ لَئِن لَّمْ تَنتَهُوا لَنَرْجُمَنَّكُمْ وَلَيَمَسَّنَّكُم مِّنَّا عَذَابٌ أَلِيمٌ ﴿18﴾

They said, 'Indeed we take you for a bad omen. If you do not desist we will stone you, and surely a painful punishment will visit you from us.'

Indeed, we take you for a bad omen; In Surah A'arāf, Allah states that 'we did not send a prophet to any town without visiting its people with stress and distress so that they might entreat [for Allah's forgiveness]' (7:94). Apparently, the messengers stayed in the city for some time and because of the abstinence of the people, the town was struck by certain calamities. A group of exegetes have described how rain did not fall in their area for some time and that the farms and harvests suffered from drought. Others say that people thought it meant that any bad incident that happened in the city, such as a fire or illness, was due to the presence of the messengers who had committed blasphemy against their gods.

This misconception has been consistent throughout the history of the prophets, including the people of Egypt who 'if something evil afflicted them, they took it as an omen connected with Moses and whoever was with him,' (7:131) and the hypocrites of Madinah who are described as 'if something bad happens to them, they say, this is because of you.' (4:78)

If you do not desist we will stone you and surely a painful punishment will visit you from us; *Rajm* used in the verse for stoning has two different meanings. It can mean stoning and it can mean swearing. Some exegetes have taken the second meaning; they argue that 'surely a painful punishment will visit you from us' would make no sense if *rajm* here means stoning.

Others have taken *rajm* to mean stoning as a way of painful punishment for the messengers. The latter meaning is more plausible as the threat of being sworn at would not intimidate the messengers. Apparently, the situation in the city did not allow the authorities to punish the messengers for simply preaching their message. Thus, they resorted to the excuse that the messengers were bringing bad luck by annoying the gods, and gave the messengers an ultimatum - either desist or be punished.

$$\text{قَالُوا طَٰٓئِرُكُم مَّعَكُمْ أَئِن ذُكِّرْتُم بَلْ أَنتُمْ قَوْمٌ مُّسْرِفُونَ} \; \langle 19 \rangle$$

They said, 'Your bad omens attend you. What! If you are admonished.... Indeed, you are an unrestrained lot.'

The answer of the messengers is clear and powerful. They deny that good or bad omens exist; a person's share of good or bad is determined by what they do; a person's actions are their bad omen.

Indeed, you are an unrestrained lot; *Musrif* is translated here as unrestrained. *Isrāf* means to lack restraint and transgress the limits; it may be limits of justice, limits of truth, limits of one's freedom, or limits of consumption. It is this latter meaning of consumption which we usually understand regarding *isrāf*. However, for this meaning the Qur'an uses the term *tabthīr* rather than *isrāf*, as in the verse: 'Give the relatives their due right, and the needy and the traveller, but do not squander wastefully (*tabthīr*).' (17:26) Therefore, *musrif* is someone who commits grave sins by transgressing the set limits of human action. Thus,

Firawn is described as a *musrif* (10:83). Therefore, the verse would mean: your bad omen is with you, if you could understand, but you do not understand because you are transgressors.

وَجَآءَ مِنْ أَقْصَا ٱلْمَدِينَةِ رَجُلٌ يَسْعَىٰ قَالَ يَٰقَوْمِ ٱتَّبِعُوا۟ ٱلْمُرْسَلِينَ ﴿20﴾

There came a man hurrying from the city outskirts. He said, 'O my people! Follow the apostles!

There came a man hurrying from the city outskirts; This man is introduced by most of the commentators as Ḥabīb al-Najjār (Ḥabīb the Carpenter). It is said that during his early meetings with the messengers, he recognized the truth of their mission and the righteous personalities; this shows that he was a man of learning and contemplation. As soon as he learnt that the messengers were in danger he rushed to the city to defend them.

Addressing the people as 'my people' *(yā qawmi)* shows that he was not a stranger in the city; he was from the same people, someone who was well known for his piety and integrity otherwise rushing to admonish his people had no justification. In Islamic tradition, this man is known as Ṣāḥibu Yāsīn or Mu'minu Yāsīn and he is held in high regard. He is said to have lived near a gate of the city far away from the populated area. A *hadīth* is narrated from the Prophet (s) in *al-Sīrah* of Ibn Hishām saying,

سُبّاقُ الأمم ثلاثة؛ لم يكفروا بالله طَرفةَ عين: حِزقيلُ مؤمن آل فرعون، وحبيب النجّار صاحب يس، وعليّ بن أبي طالب.

The forerunners of the nations are three, they did not disbelieve in God even a blink. Ḥizqīl Mu'minu Āl-e Firawn, Ḥabib al-Najjār Ṣāḥibu Yāsīn, and Ali ibn Abi Ṭālib.

In another version of the *hadīth* it is added that they were *ṣiddīqūn*, the most truthful ones. This narration is reported in different expressions yet each one demonstrates that this carpenter was a highly learned man of faith and was the first person who acknowledged those messengers.

According to the reports, the messengers met Ḥabīb when they were going to the city and he submitted to their message immediately. As he was living in the suburbs, he was not involved in the arguments and the ensuing quarrels with the messengers, but as soon as he heard they were going to be put to death he rushed to the city and supported their cause. The way he is quoted in the Qur'ān supports the narrations that imply he was one of the *ṣiddīqūn*. We can infer that Ḥabīb had a good reputation with the people of the city and was held in high regard for his piety and integrity. He hoped that the people would listen to him and desist in opposing the messengers; that is why he said, 'Indeed I have faith in your Lord, so listen to me.'

His position seems to be similar to the position of Ḥizqīl, Mu'minu Āl-e Firawn who is mentioned with him in the above *hadīth*. Ḥizqīl was a dignitary of high prominence in the court of Firawn who was concealing his faith. Some narrations even say that he was the heir-apparent to Firawn. That is why he was able to stand against Firawn and object to his decision to kill Prophet Mūsā (a). The conversation reported in Surah Mu'min, demonstrates how learned this man was, and how powerfully he could speak to Firawn:

> And Pharaoh said, "Let me kill Moses, and let him invoke his Lord. Indeed, I fear that he will change your religion, or bring forth corruption in the land…" And a man of faith from Pharaoh's clan, who concealed his faith said, "Will you kill a man for saying, 'My Lord is Allah,' while he has already brought you manifest proofs from your Lord?" (40:26 and 28)

There are a lot of similarities between Ḥizqīl

Mu'minu Āl-e Firawn and Ḥabīb al-Najjār Ṣāḥibu Yāsīn. Their level was similar in terms of respect, and their fate was similar too; both of them were killed. As soon as they revealed their support for the messengers, both of them were betrayed despite previously having lots of supporters and great respect in the eyes of the people. The Qur'ān tells us that both were immediately rewarded by God. Also, the type of knowledge and insight of both were similar too. Comparing the arguments in Surah Mu'min given by Ḥizqīl and the arguments in Surah Yāsīn given by Ḥabīb, we can conclude that both men were in the rank of *ṣiddīqūn* and had some sort of inspired knowledge about God and guidance. The verses of Qur'ān support the narrations about these men.

O my people! Follow the apostles!; By saying this Ḥabīb is acknowledging that these people were not imposters and did not bring bad omen to the city, rather they were bearers of a true message from God.

﴿ اتَّبِعُوا مَن لَّا يَسْـَٔلُكُمْ أَجْرًا وَهُم مُّهْتَدُونَ ۝21 ﴾

Follow them who do not ask you any reward and they are rightly guided.'

Here Ḥabīb puts forward two proofs in support of the messengers. Firstly, they ask for no reward for conveying the message. This is a proof of their pure motivation for conveying a message that would expose them to so much danger. There is no reason for them to risk their lives and call people to the creator except their honesty and the legitimacy of their mission.

Secondly, Ḥabīb the Carpenter testified that these people 'are rightly guided.' Rightly guided, *muhtadūn*, refers to those who receive guidance directly from God rather than being guided by anyone else. Ḥabīb himself was not a rightly guided one; he did not call the people to faith himself. He was not from the *mursalīn*, rather he was from *ṣiddīqīn*. He did not have any mission and when he preached, he did not preach as a prophet or a messenger, he simply preached as someone who had received guidance from Allah. Preaching is different from an authorised calling. These two should not be confused with each other. Yet he confirmed that those rightly guided people were messengers; this much he could do.

This story teaches us that it is important to distinguish between preaching and an authorised calling. When a man of religion preaches to people, they should listen to him, but they are not required to follow him absolutely as he might have misunderstood the message conveyed by the prophets; or he might have twisted the message of the prophets through his own opinion, either intentionally, or unintentionally.

So, his preaching is valid so long as it conforms with the guidance of the rightly guided ones, those who are directly guided by God.

The Qur'ān tells us that we should not unconditionally follow someone who is guided by someone else; we should only follow them if we judge that they are conveying the guidance of the *rightly guided* ones, those who are directly guided by God. This is because if we unconditionally follow them, we are at the mercy of their misunderstandings, misjudgements, interferences with and manipulations of the message.

A *hadīth* is reported from the Prophet (s) saying, 'My companions are like stars, whichever of them you follow you are guided.' However, we know that the companions of the Prophet (s) were not directly guided by Allah; they were following the guidance of the Prophet (s), and in that they were liable of misunderstanding and misjudgements. That is why they had so many disagreements with each other after the Prophet (s). So, if this *hadīth* could be authenticated, then it would be subject to the qualifications mentioned above. This is what we can understand from Surah Yūnus too, 'Is he who guides to the truth worthier to be followed, or he who guides not unless he is himself guided? What is the matter with you, how do you judge?' (10:35)

In summary, this man who was regarded highly by his people, came forward and testified in support of the messengers; his proofs for following them were firstly because they do not ask for any reward, and secondly because they are rightly guided (*muhtadūn*). Now he pursues his argument in a different manner.

> وَمَا لِيَ لَآ أَعْبُدُ ٱلَّذِى فَطَرَنِى وَإِلَيْهِ تُرْجَعُونَ ﴿22﴾
>
> Why should I not worship Him who has originated me, and to whom you shall be brought back?

Why should I not worship Him who has originated me: This is the third argument quoted from Ḥabīb. The style of the Qurʾān is to use ellipsis wherever possible to make the text beautifully concise. This verse is one instance. In fact, his third argument is to remind people that the messengers are not calling to anything but to worship of the one who created you. 'Why should I not worship Him who has originated me' is the continuation of the argument questioning himself as well as the people. It implies that such a worship is intuitively good and should be acknowledged by every intelligent creature.

Faṭarani, 'originated me,' is different from *khalaqani*, 'created me'. *Khalq* or creation is to make something from something else, while *faṭr* is to bring something into existence out of nothing. That is why Allah is called *aḥsan al-khāliqīn* (the best of all creators) and not *aḥsan al-fāṭirīn* (the Best of all Initiators) because there is no *fāṭir* beside Allah. Man can create certain things using different materials but he cannot bring things about out of nothing. That is why the traits which people are born with and not acquired through learning are called *fiṭrah*.

And to whom you shall be brought back; Ḥabīb's argument is based on two main premises. Firstly, worshipping the creator is intuitively good, because he has initiated us, and secondly, worshipping him is necessary because we will return to him, which the people did not claim for their idols. The reason he talks about himself rather than them by saying 'why should I not worship' is probably because the people of the city had a high regard for him and were surprised that he held the same beliefs as the messengers they were planning to kill.

The idolaters had two major differences from monotheistic worship. Firstly, they did not worship God the creator although they believed in him; and secondly, they worshipped gods who were themselves created by the creator. Ḥabīb here criticises both deviations. He establishes the intuitive virtue of worshipping the creator in this verse, and rejects the worship of any god beside him in the following verse.

> ءَأَتَّخِذُ مِن دُونِهِ ءَالِهَةً إِن يُرِدْنِ ٱلرَّحْمَٰنُ بِضُرٍّ لَّا تُغْنِ عَنِّى شَفَٰعَتُهُمْ شَيْـًٔا وَلَا يُنقِذُونِ ﴿23﴾
>
> Shall I take gods besides Him? If the All-beneficent desired to cause me any distress, their intercession will not avail me in any way, nor will they rescue me.

The people believed, similar to the polytheists in Arabia, that God cannot be reached without a mediator, an intercessor, or someone who could be served in order to intercede with God for them. These mediators became as holy as God. The people of the city wanted to kill the messengers because they were denying the existence of such mediation, and were advising that servitude should be for God alone.

If the All-beneficent desired to cause me any distress, their intercession will not avail me in any way, nor will they rescue me; This is an argument which polytheists could never refute because they still believed that there was a creator for this world. The Qur'ān tells us that even the *mushrikūn* at the time of the Prophet (s) believed in Allah as the creator. 'If you ask them, "Who created the heavens and the earth, and disposed the sun and the moon?" They will surely say, "Allah." Then where do they stray?' (29:61) Yet, despite that belief, they worshipped their demigods instead of Allah.

They thought that the great God was incomprehensible, and that he was not capable of interfering with their affairs. Additionally, they thought he was so sublime, so exalted, that he never actually polluted his hands with the affairs of this world, and he had left those matters to other smaller gods, which were created by him, like Lāt, Hubal, Uzzā and others that are mentioned in the Qur'ān. They believed that these gods interceded between them and the great God. Whatever they asked from gods, was a kind of intercession between them and the great God and those gods were receiving these things from the great God and were granting it to people. Hence, they said why should we tire ourselves worshipping the great God when he is not doing anything for us, we only worship these intercessors, the gods who are directly involved with our affairs.

As a matter of fact, when verses of the Qur'ān reject *shafā'a* in an absolute sense, it refers to this type of intercession; the intercession of demigods with God for running the affairs of this world. Such idea of intercession is absolutely rejected in *Āyat al-Kursi*, which is one of the most sublime verses in the Qur'ān. It rejects any kind of intercession of anyone, of anything, of any human being, of any god, of any kind of existence between him and the affairs of this world:

Allah there is no god except him, he is the living one, the All-sustainer. Neither drowsiness befalls him nor sleep. To him belongs whatever is in the heavens and whatever is on the earth. Who is it that may intercede with him except with his permission? He knows that which is before them and that which is behind them, and they do not comprehend anything of his knowledge except what he wishes. His seat embraces the heavens and the earth, and he is not wearied by their preservation, and he is the All-exalted, the All-supreme. (2:255)

The point that Ḥabīb is making here, is that the creator has not withdrawn himself from this world, and he is the ultimate decision maker about everything. If he intends any harm for Ḥabīb, the intercession of demigods cannot benefit him. So there is no reason to worship them, 'Shall I take gods besides him whose intercession will not avail me?' Of course not, because according to their beliefs the great God would overrule and overwhelm all decisions.

In Surah al-Zumar, the Prophet (s) put forward exactly the same argument against the *mushrikūn* of Makkah:

If you ask them, "Who created the heavens and the earth?" They will surely say, "Allah." Say,

"Have you considered what you invoke besides Allah? Should Allah desire some distress for me, can they remove the distress visited by him? Or should he desire some mercy for me, can they withhold his mercy?" Say, "Allah is sufficient for me. In him let all the trusting put their trust." (39:38)

إِنِّى إِذًا لَّفِى ضَلَٰلٍ مُّبِينٍ ﴿24﴾

Indeed, then I would be in manifest error.

إِنِّى ءَامَنتُ بِرَبِّكُمْ فَٱسْمَعُونِ ﴿25﴾

Indeed I have faith in your Lord, so listen to me.'

Equating idols with the creator is the most manifest error.

The term *rabb*, translated here as Lord, is a widely-used term in the Qur'ān and is one of the most manifest attributes of God. It means someone who looks after the affairs of another; who sustains them; cherishes them; and gives benefits and blessings to them. In this sense, the creation, according to the Qur'ān, has no *rabb* but Allah. He has no partner in Lordship (*rubūbīyyah*) as he has no partner in creation. He is *Rabb al-ʿĀlamīn* (the Lord of everything and everyone). That is why despite the belief of the polytheists who believed in the lordship of their idols, Ḥabīb here calls him their 'Lord' saying, 'Indeed I have faith in your Lord.'

Several commentators have disagreed about the addressees of this statement; some say it is the messengers while others say it is the people. Those who believe that the addressees are the messengers refer to the phrase 'your Lord.' They say that the people of the city who were polytheists did not believe that the creator *al-Raḥmān* was their Lord, rather they believed in the lordship of their idols. Therefore, this statement must have been addressed to the messengers. If we accept this interpretation then the phrase 'listen to me' (*fasma'ūn*), means 'bear witness for me'. However, this shift in address is not necessary and is against the flow of the text.

As mentioned above, by calling *al-Raḥmān* their Lord, Ḥabīb is trying to uphold his point by negating the lordship of anyone but God. Based on this, the phrase 'listen to me' (*fasma'ūn*), means accept my word and follow me.

قِيلَ ٱدْخُلِ ٱلْجَنَّةَ قَالَ يَٰلَيْتَ قَوْمِى يَعْلَمُونَ ﴿26﴾

He was told, 'Enter Paradise!' He said, 'Alas! Had my people only known

---

The Qur'ān compresses the story so that the next verse conveys that the people rejected and eventually killed Ḥabīb, and he was immediately admitted into Paradise by this statement from the angels. The details of his execution do not seem to be of importance here. What is important are the consequences of this act both for him and for his people. Moreover, nothing is said about the fate of the messengers. Early commentators have tried to fill the information gap by providing some details. For example, it is reported from Ibn Mas'ūd that "they trampled upon him with their feet until he died." Qatādah said that "they stoned him to death," while it is reported from Mujāhid and al-Ḥasan al-Baṣri that "when they decided to kill him, God lifted him up to Paradise." All these seem to be speculations as these scholars have not provided any source for their views.

He was told, 'Enter Paradise!'; The Paradise mentioned here is the Paradise of *barzakh* not the eternal Paradise, because people can only enter the eternal Paradise after the *ākhirah* sets in and the present worlds are destroyed. This can only happen after the two blows of the Trumpet, the destructive blow and the reviving blow. Between the two Trumpets are billions of years of evolution of the world. This is why those scholars like Mujāhid and al-Ḥasan al-Baṣri who have said "when they decided to kill him, God lifted him up to Paradise," have also added that "he will not die until the perishing of the Heavens and the destruction of the Paradise," and that "the Paradise that he was admitted to is susceptible to destruction."

The existence of Paradise and Hell in *akhirah* is established, and there is a Paradise and Hell in *barzakh* too. Interestingly, in this story the entrance of the believing person to the Paradise of *barzakh* is mentioned while in the story of Mu'mim- e Āl-e Firawn nothing is said about Ḥizbīl, rather entrance to Hell is mentioned for his killers:

> Then Allah saved him from their evil schemes, while a terrible punishment besieged Pharaoh's clan; the Fire, to which they are exposed morning and evening. And on the day when the Hour sets in Pharaoh's clan will enter the severest punishment. (40:45-46)

It is clear that 'the Fire, to which they are exposed morning and evening,' is not the eternal fire which will be their punishment *when the Hour sets in.*

Based on the teachings of the Qur'ān, the eternal Paradise and Hell involve a physical existence; our physical bodies will be restored before we are placed in Hell or Paradise in *ākhirah*. However, after death and before Resurrection, there is no physical life. The world of *Barzakh* is an imaginal world and hence the Hell and Paradise in that realm would be imaginal too. 'Imaginal' does not mean imaginary. On the contrary, it is more real than this world. Imaginal means that things there have no mass although they have image and dimension. It is free from the weight of mass, but full of life and colourful existence. Our souls leave this world in an imaginal body tailored to live in the imaginal and wondrous world of *barzakh*.

He said, 'Alas! Had my people only known; There is a barrier between the imaginal world in which we live after we die and the world of mass in which we currently live. In the Qur'ān, this barrier is called *barzakh*; hence the world of the dead is called the world of *barzakh*. People who die and pass through this barrier and enter the imaginal world are astonished by the wonders of that realm, especially if they are given special blessings for their good nature. This verse states that after Ḥabīb was killed and he entered the other realm, he encountered such a wonderful world and was so joyful of the blessings he received from God that he wished he could come back and inform his people about it so that they would awaken to the message.

We cannot see our loved ones after they pass away and go to the other side of this existence, but sometimes we wish to see them and know where they are in order to tell them what is happening to us. This verse shows that sometimes our deceased wish we could see them; they also want to tell us things, but they cannot. Apparently, the immediate feeling of the people who see the grace of God after they pass away, and after they see the vastness of the other side of this thick curtain which separates the two worlds, is that they want to describe that realm to us.

When we go to the other side, life expands immensely and our existence will enhance in a way that we cannot imagine. Seeing that wondrous life, we would like to tell our children and our loved ones about it. We would like to remind them that they must work for this; that there is no purpose beyond this. It is reported that when Imam Ali (a) was passing away and the veils were lifted for him he said, *'li mithli hādhā fal ya'mal al-'āmilūn'* 'Let all the workers work for the like of this!' (37:61) He wished well for his people while he was alive, but he also wished them well after they killed him. He wished they knew the reality of the life of this world so that they would desist from their ignorance and prosper as he prospered.

This approach is mentioned in Surah Āl-e Imrān about the martyrs with some difference. When the martyrs pass to the other realm and they are immediately received graciously by God, they will rejoice because those who are going to be martyred like them will receive great blessings. They cannot go back and tell them, but they are happy for them:

> Do not suppose those who were slain in the way of Allah to be dead; rather they are living and provided for near their Lord, exulting in what Allah has given them out of His grace, and rejoicing for those who have not yet joined them that they will have no fear, nor will they grieve. (3:169-170)

بِمَا غَفَرَ لِى رَبِّى وَجَعَلَنِى مِنَ ٱلْمُكْرَمِينَ ﴿27﴾

for what my Lord forgave me and made me one of the honoured ones!'

Ḥabīb received two favours from his Lord after his death which he wished his people knew about. One was forgiveness (*maghfirah*) and the other was that he was made one of the honoured ones (*mukramīn*). In his *tafsīr*, *Mafātīḥ al-Ghayb*, Fakhr al-Dīn al-Rāzi states that these two, forgiveness and honour, are necessary consequences of faith and righteous deeds. 'So that he may reward those who have faith and do righteous deeds. For such there will be forgiveness and an honourable provision.' (34:4)

For what my Lord forgave me; In Arabic two terms are used for forgiveness, one is *'afw* and the other is *maghfirah*. Although we translate both these terms as forgiveness, there is significant difference between the two. That is why in Surah Baqarah (2:286) we ask both of them from God, وَ اعْـفُ عَنَّا وَ اغْفِرْلنا 'Excuse us and forgive us.' *'Afw* is to excuse someone from the wrong they have done, but *maghfirah* is, in addition to that, is to remove any bad feeling which the wrong may have left in the heart. *Maghfirah* means to cover and hide; so Allah covers and hides the evil consequences that prevent us from receiving his blessings. Everyone is in need of *maghfirah* in order to receive God's blessings no matter how high their spiritual status.

Even our Prophet (s) was instructed to ask for *maghfirah* from Allah, 'then celebrate the praise of your Lord, and plead to him for forgiveness (*maghfirah*).' (110:3) Asking for *maghfirah* does not necessarily mean that the person has done any wrong, rather the nature of human life necessitates many shortcomings that need to be compensated in order to receive certain lofty blessings from God. That is why before entering Paradise every believer receives *maghfirah* from Allah. 'For those who have faith and do righteous deeds there will be forgiveness (*maghfirah*) and a great reward.'

(35:7) And that is why Ḥabīb, despite being one of the *siddīqīn*, informs us about the *maghfirah* that he has received from his Lord.

And made me one of the honoured ones; Anyone who enters Paradise is honoured by God. It is an honour and dignity which is unending. That is why Ṭabrasi states in *Majmaʿ al-Bayān* that 'made me one of the honoured ones,' means 'made me enter Paradise'. Living in Paradise means living close to God, in his neighbourhood, so to speak. There is no honour that is equal to that. True and real nearness to God cannot be attained anywhere but in Paradise, hence it would be a contradiction for someone to say that they want Allah but *not* Paradise.

It is only in Paradise that a deep experience of God is made possible and his breath-taking manifestations are visible by the heart. Here, the Paradise of *barzakh* and the eternal Paradise are honourable in their own right, although the experiences in the Paradise of *barzakh* are lower in rank and quality because of the lower nature of *barzakh* in terms of existence and strength.

Some commentators have adopted a more specific meaning to 'the honoured ones.' They say that 'the honoured ones' are a group of people and angels specifically mentioned in the Qurʾān for their outstanding qualities. Therefore Ḥabīb wishes to tell his people after he is killed that Allah has ennobled him by admitting him into this host of 'the honoured ones' who range from angels to chosen human beings.

Regarding these angels, we read in Surah Anbīyā' 'They say, "The All-beneficent has taken offspring." Immaculate is he! Rather they are his honoured servants. They do not venture to speak ahead of him, and they act by his command.' (21:26-27) In fact, these angels are so close to God and so high in their ranks that people thought they were children of God, while they are only honoured servants (*'ibādun mukramūn*). Regarding the purified (*mukhlasūn*) among the human beings, we read in Surah Ṣāffāt, 'and you will be requited only for what you used to do, [all] except Allah's exclusive servants. For such there is a known provision, fruits and they will be held in honour.' (37:39-42)

A final note about this verse is that 'Allāmah Ṭabrasi observes that this verse proves the existence of blessings and pleasures in the grave because Ḥabīb is saying this while his people are still alive and the world has not yet ended. By the grave, he means the realm of *barzakh*. Allāmah observes that if the existence of bliss in the grave is permissible, so is the existence of the punishment. Hence the verse invalidates the belief of Muʿtazilī in rejecting the punishment of the grave.

وَمَآ أَنزَلْنَا عَلَىٰ قَوْمِهِ مِنۢ بَعْدِهِۦ مِن جُندٍ مِّنَ ٱلسَّمَآءِ وَمَا كُنَّا مُنزِلِينَ ﴿28﴾

After him We did not send down on his people a host from the sky, nor We would have sent down.

After this man was killed, a grave punishment befell his people. We are not told what happened to the messengers, if they left afterwards or if they were killed. It seems in the context of this story, that the fate of the messengers is secondary. Here we can infer that rejecting and persecuting the messengers bring destruction, and if someone of true faith is killed unjustly and for supporting the truth, then punishment may follow.

A host from the sky; *Samā'* translated here as 'sky' is used in the Qur'ān in different ways. Literally it means anything which is raised up. Therefore, it is used for things which are physically above us, such as the skies, 'Say, observe what is in the heavens (*samāwāt*) and the earth,' (10:101); clouds, 'And we send down from the sky salubrious water,' (50:9); layers of earth atmosphere, 'we made the sky a preserved roof,' (21:32); or even a ceiling, 'Whoever thinks that Allah will not help him (the Prophet) in this world and the Hereafter, let him extend a rope to the ceiling (*samā'*) and hang himself, and see if his artifice would remove his rage.' (22:15)

Samā' is also used for things which are metaphorically raised, like realm of God 'Are you secure that he who is in the sky (*samā'*) will not unleash upon you a rain of stones?' (67:17); or abode of the angels, 'How many an angel there is in the Heavens (*Samā'*) whose intercession is of no avail in any way except after Allah grants permission.' (53:26)

Here, Heaven means the realm of angels. So, the verse means that after Ḥabīb was killed, God did not need to send a host of angels from the Heaven to destroy them.

Nor We would have sent down; Means hosts of angels were not sent down for previous nations either. The matter was much easier for Allah than that.

إِن كَانَتْ إِلَّا صَيْحَةً وَاحِدَةً فَإِذَا هُمْ خَامِدُونَ ﴿29﴾

It was but a single Cry, and, behold, they were stilled [like burnt ashes]!

It was only one single blast and they were silenced; no troops from Heavens were needed, the people were too insignificant for that. They were put out by a single blow. The verse does not go into detail about the nature of the blast or the cause of the 'cry'. It could have been the sound of a thunderbolt which came down on the city and destroyed everything, or a blast caused by a horrible earthquake ripping the earth, or a meteor darting down on their city extinguishing the life completely. The method is not significant. Rather, the Qur'ān emphasises the way in which man with all his arrogance and vainglory is weak and defenceless in the face of a single 'cry'.

Using the term *khāmidūn* (extinguished) is highly eloquent here. They are likened to a burning fire in their rage and lust. It was their lust and passion for the ware of this world that stopped them from listening to the messengers and it was their rage and anger which drove them to kill a righteous man. When the punishment came, all that fire was put out and they became like extinguished ashes.

The people of this city were destroyed completely for killing a believer who stood up for truth, and in the case of Thamūd, a whole civilization was annihilated for killing the she-camel that was carved for them as a miracle out of a rock. On the other hand, the Banū Israel killed so many prophets and yet they were not destroyed. Moreover, the Muslims killed Ḥusayn ibn Ali (a) who was certainly greater than Mu'min Āl-e Yāsīn, yet they flourished. There is an apparent inconsistency in their treatment.

One might argue that destruction comes when there is unanimity in defiance. If a whole nation unanimously opposes the truth or a sign offered to them by the messengers and their small group of followers, then they bring destruction upon themselves. Where there is no unanimity, and people have different views and affiliations, then only the opponents and culprits are punished, not by physical destruction, but by spiritual devastation. Like the case of Banū Israel whose hearts hardened and they brought a spiritual curse for themselves. 'Because of them breaking their covenant, we have cursed them, and made their hearts become hardened.' (5:13) This is a general principle which runs in all nations.

يَاحَسْرَةً عَلَى ٱلْعِبَادِ مَا يَأْتِيهِم مِّن رَّسُولٍ إِلَّا كَانُوا بِهِ يَسْتَهْزِءُونَ ﴿30﴾

How regrettable of the servants! There did not come to them any apostle but that they used to deride him.

This statement could be a continuation of Ḥabīb's words after he entered Paradise or, more plausibly, it could be a statement from God exposing the pitiful ignorance and obstinacy of the people. The latter view is the opinion of majority of the exegetes and suits with the flow of the text.

In a sense, this verse summarises the history of the encounter of messengers with their people. The general trend shows how messengers have been derided and ridiculed by their nations. One of the main concerns of our Prophet (s) when he was about to disclose his mission to the public was the contempt that he knew he was going to face. Allah knew that he needed spiritual support for that, hence he reassured him saying, 'Proclaim what you have been commanded, and turn away from the polytheists. Indeed, we will suffice you against the deriders.' (15:94-95)

At times, Allah consoled the Prophet (s) by reminding him that 'Messengers were certainly derided before you; but those who ridiculed them were besieged by what they had been deriding' (21:41). The reason for this contempt is that people are immersed in their physical senses in such a way that anything beyond that seems irrational and strange to them. The easiest way to circumvent an argument is to deride and ridicule it. This makes their situation pitiful and regrettable.

This story ends here, however, before moving on it is worth mentioning the style of historical reports in the Qur'ān. Often the Qur'ān does not proceed in a linear fashion through a story but leaps backwards and forwards in time, only mentioning the important parts. I call it, 'peak connection'; instead of telling the story from beginning to the end, the Qur'ān weaves together the important details in the story and leaves out anything irrelevant. Here, the story jumps from 'I have faith in your Lord, so listen to me' to 'he was told, "Enter Paradise!"'

These are two peak moments of the story which are joined together. What goes in between is not necessary or important to mention; they did not listen to him, they probably warned him, rebuked him, imprisoned him, tortured him and eventually killed him in a gruesome manner, but these details are not conducive to the wisdom that the report is trying to pass on to the audience, and that is way they are not mentioned. This is the most beautiful style for a book of wisdom. We must be aware of this style when we read the stories of the Qur'ān, otherwise we get lost. We can see the whole life history of Prophet Yūsuf (a), for example, reported in a short chapter in the Qur'ān. That is made possible because only those parts are mentioned which gives the reader a lesson, although by joining together the peak points we gather a concise account of his whole life.

Another beautiful example of this style is found in Surah al-Qamar with its mesmerising rhythm and rhyme when Allah recounts the story of Thamūd:

The people of Thamūd denied the warnings, and they said, "Are we to follow a lone human from ourselves?! Indeed, then we would be in error and madness. Has the Reminder been cast upon him from among us? Rather he is a self-conceited liar." Tomorrow they will know who is a self-conceited liar. We are sending the She-camel as a trial for them; so, watch them and be steadfast. And inform them that the water is to be dispensed between them; every drinking will be [fairly] attended. But they called their companion, and he complied and hamstrung her. So how were my punishment and my warnings?! We sent against them a single Cry, and they became like the dry sticks of a corral builder. Certainly, we have made the Qur'an simple for the sake of admonishment. So is there anyone who will be admonished? (54:23-32)

On reading stories like this, with such a powerful literature and penetrating tone, one might sympathise with those who used to call it magic.

أَلَمْ يَرَوْا كَمْ أَهْلَكْنَا قَبْلَهُم مِّنَ ٱلْقُرُونِ أَنَّهُمْ إِلَيْهِمْ لَا يَرْجِعُونَ ﴿31﴾

Have they not regarded how many generations We have destroyed before them who will not come back to them?

Have they not regarded; *alam yaraw* could be translated as 'have they not regarded or had they not regarded.' If we translate it as the latter, then the pronoun *they* would refer to the people of the city; meaning they rejected the messengers and killed the righteous man; 'had they not regarded' what we had done to previous generations? But if we translate it as the former, then it is a general observation for all people, especially for the people of Makkah. Sheikh Ṭūsi has adopted this latter opinion, while al-Rāzi has confirmed both meanings as probable.

...how many generations We have destroyed; We can take great lesson from the multitudes of nations who were wiped out before them. Wiping out a generation may simply refer to the natural process of life and death, or it could refer to the destruction of nations because of their misdeeds. Countless generations have passed before us with the same hope and fear, love and hate, greed and desire; all of whom are now silenced. We are linked in this unending chain and we will soon be silenced too.

The Qur'ān tells us that many nations were destroyed due to their irreversible evil conduct, and losing their purpose in life. This is based on a belief that humans have purpose in life beyond this realm otherwise the destruction of nations resembles the revenge of an angry God. This is not the case, rather, God's anger is caused by his mercy, *yā man sabaghat raḥmatuhū ghaḍabah,* 'O the one whose mercy precedes his wrath.' Leaving communities alone to go against the ultimate purpose of human life, means that any new life born to that community would be compelled to end up in perdition and this is against the mercy of God. One substantial caveat should be made here. This is a right only reserved for God, and humans are never allowed to play God in this respect. It is God who knows the purpose of life, it is he who gives life and he who takes life alone.

Who will not come back to them; Depending on how the pronouns in this phrase are understood, there are two different interpretations here. One way is to understand that those who are destroyed do not return to the living; the other way is that those who are living do not return to the dead. The first interpretation means that after they perished and left this world, they could not return back to redress their mistakes or recompense their misfortunes; there was no second chance for them. The second interpretation denotes that the destroyed generations were uprooted in such a way that they did not leave any descendent behind, and there is no living person whose lineage traces back to them. The first meaning is more popular among the exegetes and fits with the following verse.

وَإِن كُلٌّ لَّمَّا جَمِيعٌ لَّدَيْنَا مُحْضَرُونَ ﴿32﴾

And all of them will indeed be presented before Us.

Even though they cannot come back to this world; they have not perished or lost their existence; they will all be gathered before God one day. It may also mean that although they seem to be destroyed, everything is present to God. The latter meaning refers to the present and the former refers to the future on the Day of Judgment.

These verses contain many admonitions: that the path of defying God and forgetting the purpose of life leads to destruction in this world. In addition to that they will be brought to the presence of the Lord in the next world and will be questioned about what they used to do.

$$\text{وَءَايَةٌ لَّهُمُ ٱلْأَرْضُ ٱلْمَيْتَةُ أَحْيَيْنَٰهَا وَأَخْرَجْنَا مِنْهَا حَبًّا فَمِنْهُ يَأْكُلُونَ ﴿33﴾}$$

> A sign for them is the dead earth, which We revive and bring forth grain out of it, so they eat of it.

Three compelling signs are mentioned in the next set of ten verses. The surah began with the strong confirmation of the mission of the Prophet (s), then explained that the majority of them do not believe because 'the Word' has been realized on them, but they should not think that they are left unchecked. God is recording what they do and they will meet the consequences of their acts in this world and in the next. 'Indeed, we revive the dead and write what they have sent ahead and their effects, and we have figured everything in a manifest *Imām*.' (36:12) Then an example was cited for them to bring to their attention the result of their denial; they may be destroyed without the need of any troops to be sent from Heaven. This is the outcome of their obstinacy in this world.

Now before moving on to mentioning what consequences befall them in the next life, three sets of signs of God's power and mercy are brought forward.

A sign for them is the dead earth, which We revive; A decisive proof that God can give life to dead objects is the dead earth to which he gives life. Giving life is a mysterious and awesome phenomenon experienced by the intellect. It is not exactly known how inanimate beings changed into living cells, or how the seeds of plants and vegetables have been so minutely built and yet they begin to grow and absorb particles of the dead land and give them life.

According to the Qur'ān, God is the only living being from whom all life emanates. This is what we read in *Āyat al-Kursi,* 'Allah there is no god but him, the only Living one, the All-sustainer.' (2:255) Thus, the life which we see on the earth does not come from nothing. When we look at the chain of causes and effects, we see the immediate cause and the immediate effect of everything. But the Qur'ān tells us to look deeper and find a source which gives freshness and life to everything, every year, every season. Deep thought and reflection will make us realise that life on earth is a real sign of God.

The term used for *sign* here is *āyah*. *Āyah* in the Qur'ān is used in different ways depending on the context. Here, *āyah* means a sign. A verse of the Qur'ān is also called an *āyah* because it is a sign that guides us. A third meaning of *āyah* used in the Qur'ān very frequently is miracle, because again it is a sign.

When we read in different verses of the Qur'ān that the *mushrikūn* asked the Prophet (s) to bring them an *āyah*, they were asking for a miracle. 'The faithless say, "Why has not some *āyah* been sent down to him from his Lord?" You are only a warner, and there is a guide for every people' (13:7) Here, *āyah* cannot refer to a verse since the Prophet (s) brought plenty of verses to them, rather it means a miracle. Another example is, 'And should their aversion be hard on you, find, if you can, a tunnel into the ground, or a ladder into sky, that you may bring them an *āyah*.' (6:35) The fourth meaning of *āyah* is a proof, 'And if you come to those who have been given the scripture with every *āyah* they will not follow your *qiblah*' (2:145).

In the verse we are discussing here, *āyah* means a sign. The question is whether it is a sign for the Day of Judgement or a sign for the existence of God. Apparently, both are possible in this specific verse. However, the three sets of verses together are a strong reminder of the authority of Allah, his wisdom, his knowledge, his purposefulness, and his kindness.

Signs are needed because the experience of God is gradual and progressive. The first experience of God is an invocation of him by seeing his signs. When children ask about God, we refer them to what they see around them. We draw their attention to the amazing creations, such as a human beings; how they grow, how they are created, what kind of abilities they are given, how meticulously their body is organised, how harmoniously everything works in them. With respect to knowledge about God, almost all of us are like children. So initially when we talk about God, we use reasoning which supports a vague intuitive knowledge of him somewhere inside us.

However, this is not the only knowledge we can have about God. We should leave this stage behind us and progress in our *ma'rifah*. In Dua 'Arafah there is a very compelling statement by Imam al-Ḥusayn (as) at the end of a long and elating heart-to-heart with God, which alludes to that higher level of perception of God. A level that leaves the signs behind and moves on to the heart of the knowledge. He says:

كَيْفَ يُسْتَدَلُّ عَلَيْكَ بِمَا هُوَ فِي وُجُودِهِ مُفْتَقِرٌ إِلَيْكَ؟ اَيَكُونُ لِغَيْرِكَ مِنَ ٱلظُّهُورِ مَا لَيْسَ لَكَ حَتَّىٰ يَكُونَ هُوَ ٱلْمُظْهِرَ لَكَ؟ مَتَىٰ غِبْتَ حَتَّىٰ تَحْتَاجَ إِلَىٰ دَلِيلٍ يَدُلُّ عَلَيْكَ؟ وَمَتَىٰ بَعُدْتَ حَتَّىٰ تَكُونَ ٱلْآثَارُ هِيَ ٱلَّتِي تُوصِلُ إِلَيْكَ؟

How can you be figured out through that whose existence relies on you? Can anything other than you have a (kind of) manifestation that you lack and thus it may act as an indicator for you? When have you ever been absent so that you may need a sign to lead to you? When have you ever been far-off so that traces may lead to you?

He says, all these things that we see around us; the sun, the moon, the day and night, animals, plants, humans with all their love, hate, affection and mercy, are all in need of God in their existence. Therefore, how are we going to reason for his existence with these things? He is much more manifest than these things are in themselves. Why should we draw on other things when we want to talk about 'you'?

To understand God in this way requires a high degree of faith which yields true knowledge of God. Before reaching that stage, we can only know him through his signs. But the Imam says that God is so manifest that nothing can manifest him. This is also true. God fills the heavens and the earth with his presence and character in a way that nothing can be contradicted or contrasted with him. There is no other than him.

For example, if there was no night, you could never realise that there is light, because light is everywhere. You could not talk about light, or argue about light at all because there was nothing to contradict it and compare it against. You could not say that light exists unless through certain signs. The same is true about the presence of God. Since Allah is present everywhere, and there is nothing to limit him, we cannot sense him. He is so manifest, so present and so overwhelming, that if someone goes deeper in their faith and purity, the first thing they can see is his overwhelming presence. He cannot be seen by eyes because he is beyond physical perception, but as Imam Ali (a) said:

$$\text{لَا تُدْرِكُهُ ٱلْعُيُونُ بِمُشَاهَدَةِ ٱلْعِيَانِ وَلَكِنْ تُدْرِكُهُ ٱلْقُلُوبُ بِحَقَائِقِ ٱلْإِيمَانِ}$$

The eyes cannot catch him by physical vision but the hearts can perceive him by realities of faith.

Before arriving at this stage, we have no other way except to know him through signs; and that is why the Qur'ān repeatedly calls our attention to his signs. There is no contradiction between this and between what people of elevated faith tell us about their experience of God. There is no conflict between this and what Imam Ḥusayn (a) says in Dua 'Arafah: 'When have you ever been absent so that you may need a sign to lead to you?' He is speaking from a different perspective and from a different level of faith.

This is why Allah calls himself *al-Ẓāhir* and *al-*

Bāṭin, 'The Manifest and the Hidden.' (57:3) He is hidden because he is so manifest. There is nothing to contradict him or compare him with. There is no limit for him, and something which has no limit and measure, cannot be known and sensed. Colour is a limit set on visible objects, and when there is no colour, there is no limit, and you cannot see things. The same is with size and weight, as Imam Ali (a) says in *Nahj al-Balāghah* sermon 163:

$$\text{حَدَّ الْأَشْيَاءَ عِنْدَ خَلْقِهِ لَهَا إِبَانَةً لَهُ مِنْ شَبَهِهَا لَا تُقَدِّرُهُ الْأَوْهَامُ بِالْحُدُودِ وَ الْحَرَكَاتِ وَ لَا بِالْجَوَارِحِ وَ الْأَدَوَاتِ لَا يُقَالُ لَهُ مَتَى وَ لَا يُضْرَبُ لَهُ أَمَدٌ بِحَتَّى}$$

He set limits for things when he created them to distinct himself from their likeness. Imaginations cannot fathom him with limits and movements, or with limbs and agents. He is not subject to 'when' and no time limit can be set for him by 'till'.

So, how could such a being be sensed or known except through his signs or by the 'realities of faith'? Every feature in things which make their cognition possible is absent in him.

The next sentence in this sermon is the most interesting:

$$\text{الظَّاهِرُ لَا يُقَالُ مِمَّ وَ الْبَاطِنُ لَا يُقَالُ فِيمَ}$$

He is manifest, but it cannot be asked, "from what?", he is hidden, but it cannot be asked, "in what?"

God is hidden because he is so manifest, and if this is the case, then to talk about him, we have to talk about his signs; not because he is absent and he has put some clues on the earth so that we can be led to him; but because he is omnipresent, so that he cannot be comprehended except through his signs. It is only after our faith increases by pondering upon these signs that we can move beyond the signs and even analyse these signs by looking at him. This is the kind of knowledge which is given to the prophets and the 'friends' (*awliyā'*). They have knowledge of him, and anything that they look at is seen as dependent on him.

Their knowledge is the knowledge of *malakūt* in addition to their knowledge of *mulk*. Imam Ali (a) describes this here:

$$\text{ما رَاَيْتُ شَيْئاً اِلّا وَ رَاَيْتُ اللّهَ قَبْلَهُ وَ بَعْدَهُ وَ مَعَهُ}$$

I never have seen anything unless I have seen Allah before it, with it, and after it.

If someone looks at things from the perspective of the *malakūt*, they see God first and the creation second. We perceive things from the side of *mulk*, and we see the creation first and Allah is hidden. Hence, we have to know him through his signs. The former type of knowledge brings certitude, while the latter type of knowledge is in danger of doubt. 'Thus did we show Abraham the *malakūt* of the heavens and the earth, that he might be of those who possess certitude.' (6:75)

And bring forth grain out of it, so they eat of it; The relationship between humans and the earth is intricate. God gives life to its vegetation, grains, and fruits. 'Have you not regarded that Allah sends down water from the sky, whereupon the earth turns green? Indeed, Allah is all-attentive, all-aware.' (22:63) The green of the earth is nourishment for us and for the animals that we consume.

> So let man observe his food. We poured down water plenteously, then we split the earth into fissures, and made the grain grow in it, and vines and vegetables, olives and date palms, and densely-planted gardens, fruits and pastures, as a sustenance for you and your livestock. (80:24-32)

We are completely bound to this continuous and repetitive resurrection of the earth in the cycle of life.

When we go to a grocery shop it is worth pondering on all different types of fruits, vegetable, grains, nuts, rice, and wheat. All these are designed and created with all their different tastes, shapes and colours, by him alone. No one has helped him. He alone has designed all these foods so that we are nourished in such a luxurious way. He could have created just one sort of food and we would have been forced to eat it, but he wanted us to have the luxury of tastes.

The harmony between our creation and all other creations all over the earth is a sign of *tawḥīd* in diversity. We can eat from the earth and from other species created from the earth, and our body accepts them, digests them and is sustained by them 'so they eat of it.' This is a sign of the powerful consistency in creation.

وَجَعَلْنَا فِيهَا جَنَّٰتٍ مِّن نَّخِيلٍ وَأَعْنَٰبٍ وَفَجَّرْنَا فِيهَا مِنَ ٱلْعُيُونِ ﴿34﴾

We make in it orchards of date palms and vines, and We cause springs to gush forth in it,

And we make in it orchards of date palms and vines; The previous verse highlighted the importance of grain, which is a staple food for human beings. This verse draws attention to other types of food which although not essential, are necessary. Two outstanding samples of these nutrients are mentioned here, dates and grapes; these two fruits could be dried and used in many different ways or eaten as part of a balanced meal.

The Arabic term used for date palms here is *nakhīl* (sl. *nakhl*) and for vines is *aʾanāb* (sl. *ʿinab*). The subtlety of the Arabic language here is demonstrated in this beautiful nuance of words . *ʿInab* is usually used for grapes and it is rarely used for vines, while *nakhl* is a name for the date tree the fruit of which is called *tamr*. In the case of grapes, the fruit is mentioned while for of dates, the whole tree is mentioned. Some believe the palm tree is mentioned because the fruit, the trunk, the branches and the leaves are all useful, while grape vines are usually planted for their fruit alone. The usage of plural for both signifies the numerous different species of these trees.

And we cause springs to gush forth in it; The dead land is revived by vegetation and usually requires rainfall. However, orchards and vineyards need more than rain water. They need irrigation from rivers and springs. Here, another sign of harmony in nature is brought to our attention; rain water is stored in underground reservoirs and 'gushes forth,' providing nutrients. Pay attention to how Allah talks about the springs; he caused the earth to split (*fajjarnā*) and he caused the water to gush forth. It is nature, but for the wise, nature is nothing but a permanent and continuous act of Allah.

> Have you not seen that God merges the night into the day and merges the day into the night? (31:28)

> And: It is Allah who sends the winds. Then they raise a cloud, then he spreads it as he wishes in the sky, and forms it into fragments, whereat you see the rain issuing from its midst. (30:58)

> And: Allah is the splitter of the grain and the pit. He brings forth the living from the dead and he brings forth the dead from the living. That is God! Then where do you stray? (6:95)

لِيَأْكُلُوا مِن ثَمَرِهِ وَمَا عَمِلَتْهُ أَيْدِيهِمْ أَفَلَا يَشْكُرُونَ ﴿35﴾

so that they may eat of its fruit and what their hands have cultivated. Will they not then give thanks?

So that they may eat of its fruit; In the case of grains, verse number 33 said 'so they eat of it,' because grains are staple food that all humans need. Here, since the verse is about fruit, which is an extra food supplement it says, 'so that they may eat of its fruit.'

...and what their hands have cultivated; The Arabic sentence here can bear two meanings. In *wa mā 'amilathu aydīhim*, the word *mā* can be a conjunctive in which case the verse would mean, 'so that they may eat of its fruit *and* of what their hands have cultivated.' Thus, it refers to what is made of the fruits by human food processing, including dried fruits, vinegar, and sugar. However, if we take *mā* to mean negation then the meaning would be translated as, 'while their hands have not produced it.' The exegetes are divided here, however, using verse (36:71) 'Allāmah Tabātabāi supports this latter meaning. Although, we cultivate orchards and vineyards, it is ultimately Allah who creates it with his imposing presence in nature and we should not confuse toiling with creating. 'Have you considered what you sow? Is it you who make it grow, or are we the grower?' (56:63-64) Even the trellised gardens are made by him.

> It is he who produces gardens both trellised and untrellised, and palm-trees and crops of diverse produce, olives and pomegranates, similar and dissimilar. Eat of its fruits when it fructifies, and give its due on the day of harvest, and do not be wasteful; indeed, he does not like the wasteful. (6:141)

Will they not then give thanks?; How can human beings give thanks to God? Thanksgiving is either by *reciprocating* the good that we have received or by *acknowledging* the favour. As there is nothing that anyone can give to God to reciprocate, and everything belongs to him alone, and nothing can enrich him, the only way of giving thanks to Allah, is to acknowledge his favours on us.

God does not benefit from our acknowledgement, and the only reason he demands this from us is because he wants us to benefit. By acknowledging his favours, we remember him and his love develops in our heart. This love and remembrance elevates our souls and brings us closer to his mercy and increases our longing for more favours. This is why Allah tells us 'If you are grateful, I will increase for you.' (14:7) If we are grateful, our capacity for receiving blessings increases and God's favours descend on us. In a similar verse Allah says, 'Remember me, and I will remember you, and thank me, and do not be ungrateful to me.' (2:52)

Furthermore, gratefulness is a human quality embedded in our conscience, as part of our *fiṭrah*. By offering thanks to God, we acknowledge our own 'humanness'. This is beautifully expressed in the whispered prayer in *al-Ṣaḥīfah al-Sajjādiyyah* by Imam al-Sajjād (a). He states in the first duʿāʾ of *Ṣaḥīfah*:

All thanks belong to God, for, had he withheld from his servants the knowledge to thank him for the uninterrupted kindnesses with which he has tried them, and the manifest favours which he has lavished upon them, they would have moved about in his kindnesses without praising him, and spread themselves out in his provision without thanking him. Had such been the case, they would have left the bounds of humanity for that of beastliness and become as he has described in the firm text of his Book: 'They are but as the cattle—nay, but they are further astray from the way!' (25:46) Praise belongs to God, for the true knowledge of himself he has given to us, and the thanksgiving he has inspired us to offer him.

Aside from acknowledgement, *shukr* has many practical aspects detailed in the narrations. Imam Ali (a) says:

اقل ما يجب للمنعم الّا يعصى بنعمته

The least obligation towards the giver of favours is that he is not defied against by his very favours.

This is a strong expression of practical thanksgiving. For example, God has given us eyes, a favour for which we can set no price. The least we can do to offer thanks is that we do not disobey him with our eyes. The same applies for any other favour, like life, wealth, intellect, and so on.

A similar narration is reported from Imam al-Ṣādiq (a). He says: 'Thanking the favour is to avoid prohibitions [of God].'

God would never prohibit using his blessings unless it is in a harmful way. So, the benefit of this thankfulness returns to the thanks giver. It is the same when we make a vow or take a pledge. For example, we pledge that if God grants our *ḥājāt* (wishes) we will fast for a month or give an amount of charity. Sometimes simplemindedly we think that we are benefiting God by our fasting or donation, while the spiritual benefits of acts return to us. So, we should not forget that whatever Allah has set as our duties, including thankfulness, is beneficial for us alone. 'Certainly, we gave Luqman wisdom, saying, "Give thanks to Allah," and whoever gives thanks, gives thanks only for his own sake. And whoever is ungrateful, Allah is needless, praiseworthy.' (31:12)

سُبْحَٰنَ ٱلَّذِى خَلَقَ ٱلْأَزْوَٰجَ كُلَّهَا مِمَّا تُنۢبِتُ ٱلْأَرْضُ وَمِنْ أَنفُسِهِمْ وَمِمَّا لَا يَعْلَمُونَ ﴿36﴾

Immaculate is He who has created all the kinds of what the earth grows, and of themselves, and of what they do not know.

This verse is a conclusion to the previous three verses which concerned the provisions made available for humans in this world.

Immaculate is he; is the translation of *subḥān alldhi*. The expression *subḥānAllāh* is a very common term for expressing wonder and amazement, and that is the sense in which the phrase is used here. So, the verse is conveying a sense of amazement when we think about the power and wisdom of Allah in his creation. How wondrous and amazing is the one who is capable of this creation.

In addition to that, the phrase emphasises the transcendent nature of God. He is immaculate in the sense that he does not have the features and limitations of his creation and his glory must be praised.

...he who has created all the kinds; the term translated as *kinds* in the verse is *azwāj* and is used in two ways in the Qur'ān. The first meaning is *kinds* as is used here. Based on that, the verse is drawing our attention to the diversity of the species on the earth. God is the creator of all the species from the plants, animals, human beings, and other kinds of creatures that we are yet unaware of. The second meaning is *pairs*, as is used in 'In all things we have created pairs so that you may take admonition.' (51:41) The latter meaning also fills us with wonder and amazement.

And of what they do not know; Our knowledge regarding the diversity of species is continually increasing and there are still many creatures at the bottom of the oceans or in the depths of the earth waiting to be discovered. Hence, 'and of what they do not know,' may refer to these creatures. It may also refer to creatures that may live on other planets in the universe, which is also alluded to in Surah al-Shūrā: 'And among his signs is the creation of the heavens and the earth and whatever creatures he has scattered in them, and he is able to gather them whenever he wishes.' (42:29) It may also include non-physical or semi-physical beings which are hidden from us, like the angels and the *jinn*.

$$\text{وَءَايَةٌ لَّهُمُ ٱلَّيْلُ نَسْلَخُ مِنْهُ ٱلنَّهَارَ فَإِذَا هُم مُّظْلِمُونَ ﴿37﴾}$$

> A sign for them is the night, which We strip of daylight, and, behold, they find themselves in the dark!

The Arabic term *naslakhu* translated here as stripping off, is derived from *salakha* which originally means 'taking off the skin of an animal'. It is a beautiful allegory, as if the light of the day was a white garment on the body of the night, and at the sunset it is taken off its body. The allegory also reiterates the fact that the original state of the earth is darkness, and the light is added to it from another source. It is like a garment put on by a person and when he takes it off, the natural colour of his body manifests.

And a sign for them is the night; The night itself is a sign because of its darkness; it reminds us of the bounties of God that daylight brings and makes us reflect on how dependent we are on the sun. In addition, the way that daylight is stripped away and we are exposed to the night is a sign itself.

The night, which we strip of daylight; *naslakhu minhu al-nahār* is a beautiful expression used only in this verse. This expression is not used elsewhere in the Qur'ān. The night is stripped of daylight gradually and continuously on different horizons. For example, if sunset is at 6.00 o'clock in a certain place, travelling westwards it will be 6.01pm, 6.02pm and so on. From the view point of someone in space it is as if the day is being pulled out of the night continually.

The Qur'ān has considered the movement of the earth through various vivid expressions. For example, Allah describes the continuum of day and night in Surah al-A'rāf in *āyat al-sukhrah*, 'He draws the night's cover over the day, which pursues it incessantly.' (7:54) The night eagerly and without respite follows the day and covers it with its veil. It is not something that suddenly falls upon the hemisphere, rather it is a continuous process and an unending movement. Another remarkable expression is in Surah al-Zumar:

> He created the heavens and the earth with reason. He wraps the night over the day, and wraps the day over the night, and he has disposed the sun and the moon, each moving for a specified term. Look! He is the All-mighty, the All-forgiver. (39:5)

Here the two-way process is emphasised; as the night follows the day in one hemisphere, the day follows the night in another hemisphere.

Some people have thought that the whole idea of day and night and the movement of sun and earth in the Qur'ān are expressed according to the Ptolemaic astronomy and the ancient understanding of the movement of the sun round the earth. However, considering these verses about the day and the night, shows that this is absolutely untrue. Another example in this regard is the oft-repeated concept of the day going into the night and vice versa. 'Have you not regarded that Allah makes the night pass into the day and makes the day pass into the night, and he has disposed the sun and the moon, each moving for a specified term?' (31:29) And:

> Say, O Allah, Master of all sovereignty! You give sovereignty to whomever you wish, and strip of sovereignty whomever you wish; you make mighty whomever you wish, and you abase whomever you wish; all good is in your hand. Indeed, you have power over all things. you make the night pass into the day and you make the day pass into the night. You bring forth the living from the dead and you bring forth the dead from the living, and you provide for whomever you wish without any reckoning. (3:26-27)

And, behold, they find themselves in the dark!; Here one might question whether this a sign for us to acknowledge the blessing of the day or to realise that Allah could have perpetuated the night had he wished. Interestingly, in Surah al-Qaṣaṣ Allah draws our attention to the necessity of both day and night and our reliance on both:

> Say, "Tell me, if Allah were to make the night perpetual over you until the Day of Resurrection, what god other than Allah could bring you light? Will you not then listen?" Say, "Tell me, if Allah were to make the day perpetual over you until the Day of Resurrection, what god other than Allah could bring you night wherein you could rest? Will you not then perceive?" Out of his mercy he has made for you the night and the day, that you may rest therein and that you may seek from his grace and so that you may give thanks. (28:71-73)

The night and day each have their function; as there are *ayāt* in the day there are *ayāt* in the night too. The night is a time to relax the body, contemplate, remove attachments, and calm mental activities so that we can go to God with a free and unoccupied heart. The type of worship we can offer during the night cannot be offered during the day. 'Prayer at night leaves the strongest impression on the soul and the words spoken are more consistent.' (73:6)

وَٱلشَّمْسُ تَجْرِى لِمُسْتَقَرٍّ لَّهَا ذَٰلِكَ تَقْدِيرُ ٱلْعَزِيزِ ٱلْعَلِيمِ ﴿38﴾

The sun runs on to its place of rest: That is the ordaining of the All-mighty, the All-knowing.

Day and night hinge on the sun. So, it is appropriate to mention it after day and night are mentioned. *Mustaqarr* may be a verbal noun meaning rest, or an adjective for place or time. In any case, it means that the sun will run a course until it comes to resting point or until an appointed time or place by which it is destined to stop. We know that the sun along with the whole solar system orbits around the centre of the Milky Way Galaxy. The verse is seemingly alluding to this movement of the sun which will come to an end at an appointed time. As such, taking *mustaqarr* to mean 'an appointed time' rather than 'rest' or 'residing place' seems to be more plausible.

That is the ordaining of the All-mighty, the All-knowing; The size of the sun is one million and three hundred thousand times bigger than the earth and it moves at an average velocity of 828,000 km/hr.

For the sun to move in such an accurate and consistent manner, making life possible on earth, requires great power and accurate measurement. Due to its size, heat, velocity, and internal agitation, the sun does not seem to be a controllable object, unless it is subdued by an unimaginable power. This is possible by no one save Allah, whose power and knowledge knows no limit.

Taqdīr, translated here as ordaining, in essence means measurement, and sometimes has a negative connotation. Some people think that *taqdīr* leads to lack of free will in human beings; meaning that we act by the will of God in whatever we do and he has predetermined everything. Thus, *taqdīr* is usually taken to be a concept similar to predestination. However, we should not forget that free will is also part of *taqdīr* and measurement of Allah. It is predestination, but not predetermination of what we do. It is a measurement, of how things are administered in this world and in the other world as well. However, we cannot calculate and comprehend how the freely chosen interactions of billions of men and *jinn* who have free will can be part of eternal *taqdīr* of Allah.

$$\text{وَٱلْقَمَرَ قَدَّرْنَٰهُ مَنَازِلَ حَتَّىٰ عَادَ كَٱلْعُرْجُونِ ٱلْقَدِيمِ ﴿39﴾}$$

As for the moon, We have ordained its phases, until it becomes like an old palm leaf.

We have ordained its phases; *Qaddarnāhu* is from the same root as *taqdīr*, however it has been translated here as 'designed' rather than *ordained* because of the context, although both have the same meaning.

The 'phases' (*manāzil*) referred to here are the twenty-eight phases that the moon passes before its absence in the last two nights of the lunar month. When the lunar month is thirty days, the moon is visible until the twenty-eighth night, in which the moon appears very narrow with a dim lit yellow glow. In the two remaining nights, the moon is not visible; this is the phase of the new moon (*miḥāq*).

This intricate and balanced system is a natural celestial calendar. It is through these phases that passing of the months was originally deduced by man, just as night and day are known from the sun. This phenomenon is alluded to in many other verses of the Qur'ān. 'They ask you regarding the new moons, say: "They are a timing mechanism for the people as well as for the Pilgrimage."' (2:18) And more clearly, 'It is he who made the sun a radiance and the moon a light, and ordained its phases that you might know the number of years and the calculation of time.' (10:5)

In English, eight broad phases for the moon are recognised: the new moon, waxing crescent, the first quarter, waxing gibbous, full moon, waning gibbous, third quarter, and waning crescent. The Arabs used to classify these into ten phases giving each set of three nights a name. They called the first three nights *ghurar*, the next three nights *nufal*, the following three nights *tusa'* (nine), because the last of them is the ninth of the month. Then the next three nights are called *'ushar* (ten), because the first of them is the tenth of the month. We then have the three nights of *al-bīḍ* (white), because of the light of the moon which shines brightly throughout these three nights. The next three nights are called *dura'*, the plural of *dar'ā'*, because the first part of the night is dark in these nights due to the moon rising late. The next three nights are *zulam*, then *hanādis*, then *da'ādi*, and finally *mihāq*.

Until it becomes like an old palm leaf; *'urjūn* is that part of the stem in palm branch which connects the bunch of dates to the trunk. When it is aged and dried it is curved like a crescent. Dates grow on the date palm in the form of bunches and the end of this bunch is a yellow wooden arc which is attached to the tree. When the bunch of dates is cut, that wooden arc branch remains on the tree and when it dries, it is very similar to the crescent before the new moon; it is a yellow withered arc with its tips downward. So, the simile works beautifully from different aspects. The old moon is likened to the old stem, curved, withered, with its tips drooping down in the dark sky as the *urjūn* is in the mass of green branches of the palm.

لَا ٱلشَّمْسُ يَنۢبَغِى لَهَآ أَن تُدْرِكَ ٱلْقَمَرَ وَلَا ٱلَّيْلُ سَابِقُ ٱلنَّهَارِ وَكُلٌّ فِى فَلَكٍ يَسْبَحُونَ ﴿40﴾

Neither it behooves the sun to overtake the moon, nor may the night outrun the day, and each swims in an orbit.

The orbits of the sun and the moon are calculated in a way that they never collide with each other. This is the measurement of Allah which has no disorganisation.

Those who argue that this meticulous organisation is the work of science should realise that science is human struggle to understand the intelligence already in place in creation. Studying science should add to our awe and appreciation for the intelligence imbued in creation. The more we are knowledgeable about this world; the more our science improves; the better we can grasp the signs of Allah and appreciate his *taqdīr*.

$$\text{وَءَايَةٌ لَّهُمْ أَنَّا حَمَلْنَا ذُرِّيَّتَهُمْ فِى ٱلْفُلْكِ ٱلْمَشْحُونِ ﴿41﴾}$$

A sign for them is that We carried their progeny in the laden ship,

---

The two previous sets of *ayāt* talked about the measurement of Allah in the world around and above us. This set of *ayāt* draws our attention to the security that Allah provides us on the earth. This is a totally different type of blessing. From another angle, the first set of *ayāt* told us how Allah has created everything in a way that sustains human beings on this earth. The second set of *ayāt* refer to our planet and our life on earth within a wider context of the universe. This third set of *ayāt* talks about the life itself and how securely we are sustained on earth.

...we carried their progeny; *dhurrīyyah* which is translated here as progeny is from *dharr* which means a tiny particle. The offspring of a person is called *dhurīyyah* because they come forth from tiny particles. It is used for both plural and singular. When Prophet Zakarīyā (a) was asking Allah for a son he said, 'My Lord, grant me a pure *dhurrīyyah*.' (3:38)

...in the laden ship; Ships are not only loaded with people, but with all types of luggage, goods, merchandise, animals, and recently, cars and trains. Ships are the greatest and the most important means of transport on earth. The sign referred to here is probably how the laws of nature work in unison to make it possible for us to travel on water with loaded ships without sinking or drowning. We usually take these laws for granted, while the verse implies that these are all accurately planned and measured by Allah to allow you to move around easily and quickly on the planet. The reason the verse talks about carrying their offspring rather than themselves, is because people are more concerned about their children's safety rather than their own. Despite their love for their children, they feel so secure about the constancy and dependability of Allah's creation that they send them off to sail on waters without fear.

Despite that, some commentators have inferred from the term 'offspring' that the verse refers to the Ark of Prophet Nūh (a) as they were the only offspring of Adam (a) that were carried to safety in The Great Flood. It refers to the mercy of God which saved the human race in that overwhelming deluge.

Or *durriyyah* here means their 'seed'. He saved them when they were only seeds in the loins of their ancestors, a few thousand years before they came to this world. A sign for them is that we carried them, the people who were to come into being in future, in a laden ship, filled with humans and animals, while they were only seeds in the loins of their fathers.

The main issue with this interpretation is the controversial assumption that all living beings including all humans and animals were destroyed on earth by the flood except those on the Ark. People living in other parts of the world had not rejected the call of Prophet Nūh (a), so there was no reason to destroy all the people in the world because the people of Prophet Nūh (a) rejected him.

﴿وَخَلَقْنَا لَهُم مِّن مِّثْلِهِ مَا يَرْكَبُونَ ﴿42﴾

and We have created for them what is similar to it, which they ride.

Of course, ships are not the only mode of transport Allah has created the like of which we board and ride. Al-'Awfī has reported from Ibn Abbas that, 'This means the camel, for it is the ship of the land on which they carry goods and on which they ride.' However, al-Ṭabarī has reported a different account from Ibn Abbas saying that it 'referred to the ships which were made after the Ark of Prophet Nūh, peace be upon him, which was similar to it.' This latter view was the view of most of the early commentators. This is more accurate since the verse explicitly mentions 'and we have created for them what is similar to it,' which would exclude animals since they are not similar to ships in creation; it also makes more sense, particularly considering the verse that follows. However, the reference may include chariots, wagons, coaches, and in recent times, bicycles, cars, lorries, and aeroplanes, as well as whatever will be invented by man in future. 'And horses, mules and asses, for you to ride them, and for adornment, and he creates what you do not know.' (16:8)

Allah has described himself as the maker of these vehicles in order to make us realise that anything made by us is in reality a creation of Allah who has created us, our intelligence, our power and our abilities.

$$\text{وَإِن نَّشَأْ نُغْرِقْهُمْ فَلَا صَرِيخَ لَهُمْ وَلَا هُمْ يُنقَذُونَ ﴿43﴾}$$

And if We like We drown them, whereat they have no one to call for help, nor are they rescued

And if We like We drown them; We have invented cars, lorries, ships, aeroplanes, and spacecrafts, all of which facilitates our transportation. But these all work because of the accommodating environment that God has generated for us. This is the meaning of 'if we like we drown them' and there would have been no one to call for help. This is mentioned more clearly in

Surah Shūrā. 'Among his signs are the ships that run on the sea appearing like landmarks. If he willed, he could have stilled the winds, leaving them motionless on top of the water. In that are signs for everyone who is patient, appreciative.' (42:31-32) The accommodating environment is usually taken for granted.

Our mistake is to think that whatever we build, create, and invent, is our own creation. But if oil did not burn, or if iron was not magnetic or if water did not cause things to float, our inventions would be meaningless. When we build, or produce things in this world, we are simply putting together the resources we find. We have found the qualities in atoms by which we can make atomic energy, we have not created them. We must avoid growing arrogant about our achievements and instead always remember that the blessings in this world come from God alone.

It may have been the case that for Arabs in those days, ships were the most significant product of human intelligence, but on reflection, God is alluding to all human products, all the inventions they have ever made in this world; they are all simply the same thing. 'If he willed, he could have stilled the winds, leaving them motionless.' If he wished, he would have made the qualities of atoms a bit different and there would be no atomic energy. If he willed he would not have put those qualities in the components which make silicon chips and we could not store data in them nor have computers or smart phones. Day by day, we are exploring more *barakah* on this earth. 'He has placed headlands towering above the earth and blessed whatever is in it.' (41:10)

Whereat they have no one to call for help, nor are they rescued; We are so ungrateful to God, we commit many sins against him, we have forgotten all his favours and blessings, and for all these, if he wishes he could drown us without any blame from anyone. If he does that no one will ethically object, and no one in reality can help. There will be no helper because all potential helpers are dependent on him.

This meaning is reiterated in many other verses of the Qur'ān. 'And were Allah to punish men for what they earn, he would not leave any creature on the earth, but he respites them till an appointed term.' (35:45) A very interesting *hadīth* is narrated regarding the verses 30 to 35 of Surah al-Ḥāqqah. The verses are addressed to the angels regarding any ungrateful profligate:

> Seize him, and fetter him! Then put him into Hell. Then, in a chain whose length is seventy cubits, bind him. Indeed, he had no faith in Allah, the All-supreme, and he did not urge the feeding of the needy; so, he has no friend here today. (69:30-35)

The narration says, when this command is issued by God and the angles move to seize the wicked, he would say: 'Have mercy.' The angels would reply, 'The most merciful did not have mercy on you; how can we have mercy on you?' Our mercy is just a splinter of him - it is just something bestowed on us by him. How could we have mercy upon you while he does not pity you.

There is no one more merciful than Allah; no one more just than him. So, in this case, if he decides to let you drown no one can help. Similarly, if he decides to help you, no one can prevent him.

إِلَّا رَحْمَةً مِّنَّا وَمَتَاعًا إِلَىٰ حِينٍ ﴿44﴾

except by a mercy from Us and for an enjoyment until some time.

So if we are not drowned, it is due to God's mercy not because we deserve it; and because it is destined that we live for an appointed time.

Enjoyment until some time; this phrase is mentioned in the Qur'ān in several places. The first time Allah uses this is when he addresses Adam (a). 'He said, "Get down, being enemies of one another! And on the earth shall be your abode and enjoyment [of sustenance] for a time."' (2:36) No matter how many sins the people on earth commit, and how much mischief they bring about, they can only live on earth until an appointed time. This appointed time, which is the end of human life on earth, is very short for Allah, while for us it seems very long.

Sometimes we wonder why Allah does not intervene in the world despite all the oppression, mischief, and wrongdoings. The reason is because God has appointed a time for us to enjoy the provision on earth:

> Were Allah to take mankind to task for their wrongdoing, he would not leave any living being upon it. But he respites them until a specified time; so when their time comes they shall not defer it by a single hour nor shall they advance it. (16:61)

This answers many of our questions about why Allah does not intervene in whatever happens on the earth; why for example someone kills thousands and millions of people and nothing happens; why Imam Ḥusayn (as) was killed and the world did not end: because it is not yet the appointed time.

Of course, the way we behave has some bearing on the type of blessings we receive.

If the people of the towns had been faithful and God wary, we would have opened to them blessings from the heaven and the earth. But they denied; so, we seized them because of what they used to earn. (7:96)

Also: Corruption has appeared in land and sea because of the doings of the people's hands, that he may make them taste something of what they have done, so that they may come back. (30:41)

وَإِذَا قِيلَ لَهُمُ ٱتَّقُوا مَا بَيْنَ أَيْدِيكُمْ وَمَا خَلْفَكُمْ لَعَلَّكُمْ تُرْحَمُونَ ﴿45﴾

And when they are told, 'Beware of that which is before you and that which is behind you, so that you may receive His mercy…'

This verse is the first clause of a conditional sentence while its main clause is omitted. Such an omission is a common literary device in Arabic to leave the conclusion to the reader, or to take the answer for granted, or to imply that the result is so dreadful that cannot be mentioned. Here, it indicates that their rejection is so remarkable that it needs no mention, although the following verse can act as the main clause of this conditional sentence.

Beware of that which is before you and that which is behind you; Some commentators have interpreted the two expressions to refer to how the idolaters persisted in their ignorance and the sins that they had committed in the past, 'that which is behind you,' and what was to happen to them in the future, 'that which is before you,' on the Day of Judgment or in this world. Others have said that 'that which is before you' refers to the punishment that befell previous nations and 'that which is behind you' refers to the punishment of the hereafter which will finally reach them and will encompass them.

A third view is that the verse refers to the sins that they presently commit, and the sins that they have committed in the past. It serves as a reminder to refrain from current sins, and to repent and ask for forgiveness, 'so that you may receive [his] mercy,' for sins committed in the past. Even if the most stubborn among the *kuffār* realise their mistakes, refrain from further sins, and repent for their previous actions – God will forgive them.

The cautionary 'may' is used to tell us that even if they do stop sinning and repent, they can only be hopeful and not certain about receiving God's mercy. This caution is often repeated in the Qur'ān to emphasise that there are many conditions that must be met before attaining God's mercy. One outstanding example is the verse prescribing fasting. 'O you who have faith! Prescribed for you is fasting as it was prescribed for those who were before you, so that you may be God wary.' (2:183) Here, the purpose of fasting is defined as increasing *taqwā*. However, even after fasting we only *may* increase in *taqwā*, because this depends on many other issues, like the way we perform the fast, our overall attitude, our other actions and inactions, and so on. If these conditions are met and we fast, then we can expect the desired result which is increasing *taqwā*.

There is a fourth interpretation of this verse which opens some interesting avenues for discussion. If sins are only punishable in the Hereafter, we should not fear their consequences in this world as Allah is not punishing us for our sins at the moment and we only have to fear what comes in the future; beyond this world. Considering that, the fourth interpretation discusses the idea that sins are punishable in this world also and 'that which is before you,' refers to the punishment for sins in this world and 'that which is behind you,' refers to the punishment for sins in the Hereafter.

The punishment that we see in the other world is actually an incarnation of the punishment that we are experiencing in our hearts right now. The consequences of sins are immediate. This may be the meaning of the verse which says 'Allah is swift in reckoning' (3:199);

as soon as we commit a sin, as we have in *hadīth*, a black spot appears in your heart. The black spot is the punishment which then manifests in the other world. This is because the sin distances us from God. The accumulation of these black spots on a person's heart distances them from God's special attention. On the Day of Judgment when every soul is seeking a way towards their Lord, he will not speak to some, or look at them, they will be distanced because of the evil of their sin.

A beautiful *hadīth* from Imam al-Ṣadiq (a) confirms this interpretation. He said in the explanation of the verse, 'Fear what is with you in terms of sins and what is behind you in terms of punishment.' This is why if the *awlīyā' Allāh*, who were closer to God than others, committed a *tarki 'ūlā*, an act which was not a sin but not preferred in the eyes of God, they became fearful.

So that you may receive [his] mercy; God's mercy is not like a switch that will be turned on in the next world. If we are included in his mercy here we are included there as well. It is the same thing manifested in different realms. If a person is vicious in this world, they should not expect a miracle to occur in the other world which allows them to enter Allah's mercy. In other words, everything should be completed in this world; we receive nothing in the next world except what we have sent forward from this world:

The day when every soul will find present whatever good it has done; and as to whatever evil it has done it will wish there were a far distance between it and itself. Allah warns you to beware of [disobeying] him, and Allah is most kind to his servants. (3:30)

When people see the blaze of Hell they are informed; 'That is because of what your hands have sent ahead, and because Allah is not tyrannical to the servants.' (8:51) Therefore, if someone wants to receive the mercy of God, they have to receive it in this world although that mercy would grow a million times in the other world. When a person receives God's mercy, they see a change in their desires. They do not desire this world anymore but the world beyond; they desire to worship him; they start to love him. He changes the love which is in their heart from mundane to eternal. This is like the *duʿā* that we whisper:

اللهم ارزقنى التجافى من دار الغرور و الانابة الى دار الخلود

O Allah grant me awakening from the world of deception and turning to the world of eternity.

When God wants to have mercy on us, we feel its effect in the origin of our love, our desires and our inclinations. The way we see this world transforms as per the *hadīth* that says, 'When one deserves *wilāytullāh* and blessings the death comes before the eyes and the aspirations hide behind; and when one deserves *wilāytu al-Shayṭān* and misery the aspirations come before the eyes and the death hides behind.'

$$\text{وَمَا تَأْتِيهِم مِّنْ ءَايَةٍ مِّنْ ءَايَٰتِ رَبِّهِمْ إِلَّا كَانُوا عَنْهَا مُعْرِضِينَ ﴿46﴾}$$

There does not come to them any sign from among the signs of their Lord but that they have been disregarding it.

This verse concludes the three sets of previous verses. The conclusion is that they are not going to regard any of these signs. 'How many a sign there is in the heavens and the earth that they pass by while they are disregardful of it' (12:105) In other words, this verse draws our attention to the reaction of the faithless to the signs of God and his admonitions.

> وَإِذَا قِيلَ لَهُمْ أَنفِقُوا مِمَّا رَزَقَكُمُ ٱللَّهُ قَالَ ٱلَّذِينَ كَفَرُوا لِلَّذِينَ ءَامَنُوٓا أَنُطْعِمُ مَن لَّوْ يَشَآءُ ٱللَّهُ أَطْعَمَهُۥٓ إِنْ أَنتُمْ إِلَّا فِي ضَلَٰلٍ مُّبِينٍ ﴿47﴾
>
> When they are told, 'Spend out of what Allah has provided you,' the faithless say to the faithful, 'Shall we feed someone whom Allah would feed, if He wished? You are only in manifest error.'

Allāmah Tabātabāi has a theory about faith in the Qur'ān which is applicable in this verse. He says faith has two pillars, one is belief in God, and the other is to be kind with the people. These two pillars are not mutually exclusive. You could not have faith without caring about other people and caring about other people is of no avail without having faith in God. One cannot claim to be a faithful person, and say that they fulfil their duties towards God, but ignore the poor and hungry. They cannot turn away and say "it's none of my business. God will feed them. God himself is very merciful and if he doesn't have mercy on them how could I; why should I have any mercy on them." Of course, this is not acceptable.

Imam Ali (a) has said, 'No poor would ever go hungry except because some wealthy person has their provision.'

The previous sets of verses in this surah talked about faith in God and reflecting on his signs. This verse talks about the other pillar of religion: being kind and considerate toward people, especially the poor.

This approach is repeated throughout many different verses in the Qur'ān. Here, three instances which emphasise this inseparable relation between faith in God and service to people will be explored. The first instance is from Surah al-Ḥāqqah. When Allah commands the faithless to be seized and taken to the Hell; he justifies it as follows, 'Indeed he had no faith in Allah, the All-supreme, and he did not urge the feeding of the needy, so he has no friend here today, nor any food except pus.' (69:33-36)

The second instance is from Surah al-Muddathir, when the people of Paradise question the people of Hell about what they had done to deserve Hell, 'they say: "Every soul is hostage to what it has earned, except the People of the Right Hand." They will be in gardens, questioning the guilty: "What drew you into Hell?"' (74: 38-42) The answer is very interesting and confirms what was said before. However, before examining the answer there are two interesting points worth mentioning here. The first is that the people in Paradise can converse with the people in Hell from where they are. We do not know how this is possible, except that there is a different realm with completely different laws and rules of nature. The second point is that the people of Paradise have a genuine curiosity and desire to understand how Allah has forgiven all of their wrongdoings, yet there are some whom God has not forgiven. They wonder how, despite the great mercy shown by God on Judgment Day, some have ended up in Hell.

This brings to mind an anecdote from the time of Imam Zayn al-ʿĀbidīn (a). Al-Hasan al Basri, a contemporary of the Imam (a), was a mystic who was well-known for his perspective that God was to be greatly feared. One day he said in his lecture; "There is no surprise about those who go to Hell how they go to Hell; the surprise is about those who go to Paradise, how they go to Paradise." Upon hearing this, one of the companions of Imam Zayn al-ʿĀbidīn (a) became terrified. When he went to visit the Imam (a), he was so visibly distraught that the Imam asked him what happened and he repeated the story. The Imam replied that his opinion was different. He said; "There is no surprise about those who go to Paradise how they go to Paradise; the surprise is about those who go to Hell, how they go to Hell." This means that the mercy of God on that day is so great that it is difficult to imagine how some people do not receive it.

Returning to those verses, when asked about their final abode, this is what the people of Hell say. 'They will answer, "we were not among those who prayed. Nor did we feed the poor. We used to gossip along with the gossipers, and we used to deny the Day of Retribution, until death came to us." So, the intercession of the intercessors will not avail them.' (74:43-48)

The third instance is in Surah al-Mā'ūn, which is very explicit and emphatic:

> Did you see him who denies the Retribution? That is the one who drives away the orphan, and does not urge the feeding of the needy. Woe to them who pray those who are heedless of their prayers, those who show off, but deny aid. (107:1-7)

In all these instances, and many more throughout the Qur'ān, these two pillars of religion complement each other.

Whom Allāh would have fed, had he wished; with this answer the faithless deceitfully confuse the two types of will of Allah, the existential will (*al-irādah al-takwīniyyah*) and the legislative will (*al-irādah al-tashrī'iyyah*). This is the will of Allah in the realm of creation and the will of Allah in the realm of legislation. By this fallacy, things that should be attributed to ourselves are attributed to God. For example, if we commit a sin, or if we have a shortcoming, we say if

Allah willed I would not have done such a thing. We attribute our sins to him while Allah, in his legislative will, always forbids us from committing sins. Yes, in his existential will he has ordained that we are free to follow his legislative will or to violate it. He allows our free choice with his existential will, while he becomes displeased if we use that ability to disobey his legislative will.

وَيَقُولُونَ مَتَىٰ هَـٰذَا ٱلْوَعْدُ إِن كُنتُمْ صَـٰدِقِينَ ﴿48﴾

And they say, 'When will this promise be fulfilled, should you be truthful?'

This question is posed by the disbelievers to the Prophet (s) and is quoted in the Qur'ān six times, each with a different answer. It may be useful to see all the six answers here:

- Surah Yūnus: 'And they say, "When will this promise be fulfilled, should you be truthful?" Say, "I have no control over any benefit for myself nor any harm except what Allah may wish. There is a time for every nation: when their time comes, they shall not defer it by a single hour nor shall they advance it."' (10-48-49)

- Surah al-Anbīyā': 'And they say, "When will this promise be fulfilled, should you be truthful?" If only the faithless knew of the time when they will not be able to keep the Fire off their faces and their backs, nor will they be helped!' (21:38-39)

- Surah al-Naml: 'And they say, "When will this promise be fulfilled, should you be truthful?" Say, "Perhaps right behind you there is some of what you seek to hasten."' (27:71-72)

- Surah al-Saba': 'And they say, "When will this promise be fulfilled, should you be truthful?" Say, "Your promised hour is a day that you shall neither defer nor advance by an hour."' (34:29-30)

- Surah Yāsīn: 'And they say, "When will this promise be fulfilled, should you be truthful?" They do not await but a single Cry that would seize them as they wrangle.' (36:48-49)

- Surah al-Mulk: 'And they say, "When will this promise be fulfilled, should you be truthful?" Say, "Its knowledge is only with Allah; I am only a manifest warner."' (67:25-26)

Each answer explains the issue from a different angle. The faithless were not seeking a genuine answer from the Prophet (s), rather they sought to make a mockery of the idea of resurrection; however, each time they were given a decisive answer as if the question was genuine. In this surah, following the weak pretext they made for not helping the poor, they sought to ridicule the idea of life after death.

The faithless raised two objections regarding the idea of resurrection. The first objection was regarding the power of God in bringing about the Resurrection. This objection has been powerfully and convincingly answered in the Qur'ān.

> Do they not see that Allah, who created the heavens and the earth and who was not exhausted by their creation, is able to revive the dead? Yes, indeed he has power over all things. (46:33)

> And he cites an example for us, while forgetting his own creation! He says: "Who can revive the bones while they are dust?" Say: "The one who initiated them in the first place will revive them, and he has knowledge of all creation." (36:78-79)

The second objection, as mentioned in this verse, was about the time of its occurrence. This was an irrelevant question; in fact, it was not a real question, rather a denial, but the Qur'ān respectfully provided an explanation. We, as individuals, are very short lived on this earth and the matter of Resurrection and destruction of the world is beyond the scale of our lifetime.

The point about resurrection is that it only happens once in this world; therefore, there cannot be any evidence for them from past experiences. The faithless themselves knew that there was no answer to this question, something that the Qur'ān also reiterates time and again:

> They question you concerning the Hour, when will it set in? Say, "Its knowledge is only with my Lord: none except him shall manifest it at its time. It weighs heavy on the heavens and the earth. It will not overtake you but suddenly." They ask you as if you were in the know of it. Say, "Its knowledge is only with Allah, but most people do not know." (7:187)

It happens suddenly taking everyone by surprise. Even the Prophet (s) does not know when that unique event is going to happen. Even the angels do not know, even Isrāfīl who is going to blow the trumpet to begin the process does not know when that is going to happen. This knowledge is hidden from everyone because it is not a knowledge that could be carried by any soul, 'it weighs heavy on the heavens and the earth.'

Sometimes the faithless demanded the revival of the dead as evidence. 'And when our manifest signs are recited to them, their only argument is to say, "Bring our fathers back to life, should you be truthful."' (45:25) The argument was that if the dead are going to rise; why are our fathers not revived in front of our eyes. Again, this is not a real question but a denial, since they knew that no one would be revived before the unique event overtakes the world. In fact, the Qur'ān says that the motive behind this question was not to know but to relieve themselves from the responsibility that they felt towards it. 'Does man suppose that we shall not put together his bones? Yes indeed, we are able to proportion even his fingertips! Rather man desires to go on living viciously. He asks, "When is this day of resurrection?"' (75:3-6)

Again, the Qur'ān does not leave the question without an answer and instead of fixing a time for it, the Qur'ān defines the signs that go with it. 'When the eyes are dazzled, and the moon is eclipsed, and the sun and the moon are brought together, that day man will say, "Where is the escape?"' (75:7-10) However, before these disruptions occur in the universe, before 'the sun is wound up, and the stars are scattered, and the mountains are set moving,' and 'the seas are set afire,'

(81:1-6) and before 'the sky is rent apart, and the stars are scattered, and the seas are merged,' (82:1-3) there will be no sign of it, and this is what the following verse tries to express.

مَا يَنظُرُونَ إِلَّا صَيْحَةً وَٰحِدَةً تَأْخُذُهُمْ وَهُمْ يَخِصِّمُونَ ﴿49﴾

They do not await but a single Cry that will seize them as they wrangle.

This refers to the first blowing of the trumpet when all living beings will virtually die. This first blowing entails a process of death which includes all living human beings at the time, human souls who live in *barzakh*, *jinn*, and angels. This will happen in a durable period of time, but for those who still live on the earth it is immediate and decisive according to this verse. Alternatively, narration is reported from the Prophet (s) explains:

هي ثلاث نفخات: نفخة الفزع، و نفخة الصعق، و نفخة القيام لرب العالمين

There are three blows, the blowing of fear, the blowing of swooning, and the blowing of rising for the Lord of the worlds.

Based on this narration, the verse mentioned here refers to the first blow, while the second blow makes the souls in *barzakh* and the angels in the heavens swoon. If this narration is correct, then the Qur'ān combines the first and the second blowing into one. However, this *ḥadīth* is in contradistinction with the Qur'ān which consistently talks about two blows only. It is probably made to address the problem of the people living on the earth and the people living in the Barzakh dying simultaneously. However, we have other *ḥadīth* which say that not all will die simultaneously by the first blowing, rather it will be a gradual advance of death from realm to realm.

At any rate, this *ṣayḥah* (cry) comes so suddenly that it overtakes the people while they are in the marketplaces and places of work, arguing and disputing as they usually do. According to some narrations, it occurs so unexpectedly that people who have taken some food from the plate to eat, will die before it reaches their mouths; and people who have spread a roll of fabric bargaining over its price are seized before they can roll it back.

The expression 'as they wrangle,' may refer to the wrangling in business or to the dispute over the 'promise' of Resurrection as mentioned in the previous verse.

The *ṣayḥah* (cry) referred to in this verse is the distinctive mark of the end of the world. All the messengers of God have informed us that one day this present world (*dunyā*) will come to an end and the entire world of creation will enter a new realm which is called the Hereafter (*ākhira*). The Qur'ān tells us that the end of the world will come about violently and terrifyingly such that every sentient being including the souls of human beings, the *jinn* and the angels will be stunned, 'On the day that the trumpet will be blown everyone in the heavens and the earth shall be petrified.' (27:87) In this verse, the dwellers of the heavens refer to angels and the dwellers of earth refer to mankind and *jinn*, both in the material world and in *barzakh*.

The *ṣayḥah* (cry) will create such a cataclysm that causes the earth to go through unprecedented convulsions, 'The earthquake of the final hour is a tremendous thing.' (22:1) 'The sun will be extinguished, the stars will fade and the seas will burst into flame.' (81:1-3) 'The skies will be rent asunder and the ground will be pounded to an extent that it will become featureless.' (84:1-3) All these occur in the wake of a fearsome blast of sound, which is itself the cause of the end of the world. This blast or *ṣayḥah* shall be brought forth by Isrāfīl, one of the greatest angels of God, and it will be of an unknown nature and never experienced before. The Qur'ān refers to the action of Isrāfīl as the 'blowing of the trumpet' (*nafakhat al-ṣūr*):

And when the trumpet is blown with a single blast, and the earth and the mountains are carried away and crushed with a single crushing; on that day the Great Event shall come to pass; and the heaven shall cleave asunder, and become weak [...] (69:13-16)

Obviously, the *ṣayḥah* is no ordinary loud sound, because it affects the corporeal world as well as the world of souls, and beyond that, it encompasses the angelic realm as well. No creature remains sentient in the entire cosmos, except a few who remain alive by God's will. Death encompasses all; all perceptions are silenced and the world is taken over by a total stillness and darkness. It is as if life never existed at all; indeed, God is needless of everything.

$$\text{فَلَا يَسْتَطِيعُونَ تَوْصِيَةً وَلَآ إِلَىٰٓ أَهْلِهِمْ يَرْجِعُونَ ﴿50﴾}$$

Then they will not be able to make any will, nor will they return to their folks.

This highlights how abruptly the *ṣayḥah* takes place, and how it takes everyone by surprise. No business deal can be completed, and no one can return to their families to bid them farewell. The *ṣayḥah* spares no one and gives no respite to anyone, and there remains not a single soul to hear and fulfil any will or listen to any recommendation.

وَنُفِخَ فِى ٱلصُّورِ فَإِذَا هُم مِّنَ ٱلْأَجْدَاثِ إِلَىٰ رَبِّهِمْ يَنسِلُونَ ﴿51﴾

And when the Trumpet is blown, behold, there they will be, scrambling towards their Lord from their graves!

Going back to the Lord is the final destination of everyone in this world. Our physical bodies were fashioned in the wombs, our souls were fashioned in this world, and our real life begins by returning to our creator. This begins after this world is destroyed by the first blowing of the Trumpet and after the souls are revived by its second blowing. It is after the second blowing that 'they will be scrambling from their graves towards their Lord.' Between the two blasts is absolute blankness and absence of any perception.

The complete death of the world and total stillness are a platform for the evolution of the universe into a new world. During this interval, all dimensions of the universe, from the earth to the heavens, from the realm of *barzakh* to the highest realms of the angels, evolve into a richer and more fascinating world. In that stillness of life, the universe is in the all-capable hands of God. With his infinite love and care, he prepares, in the absence of all living beings, the ground for their return to a richer life and a more expansive world, so that they can continue on their journey towards him.

No one shall exist to measure or appreciate the duration of this lifeless silence. It is for this reason that when everyone returns to life again, they think that no more than a few hours or days have passed. In truth, what has actually occurred during their stasis is an evolution that has lasted longer than the age of creation. Billions of years will pass before the world assumes its final form, ready to be inhabited by man and other creatures for eternity. During this process, God in his mercy has placed all his creatures in a deep slumber to protect them from the tumultuous and violent changes as the universe transforms and rejuvenates itself.

The second blast or blowing of the trumpet will also be executed by Isrāfīl. However, this is no longer the same Isrāfīl who blew into the trumpet that caused the death of creation, rather he is the Isrāfīl who has been resurrected by God in the realm of the afterlife. With his enhanced form, he grasps the trumpet of life, and as he blows into it, by God's command the breeze of life enters every atom in creation and enlivens every dead being, angel, *jinn*, man and animal.

Scrambling towards their Lord from their graves; The use of the verb *yansilūn*, 'scramble', indicates the swiftness with which the process of returning to the Lord will take place. The term *ajdāth* used in the verse is the plural of *jadath*, which means grave. This and countless other verses of the Qur'ān imply that there is a physical aspect to the Resurrection beside its spiritual aspect and that man's newly formed body will be made of the same former materials. 'Does man think that we shall not reassemble his bones? In fact, we are able to restore his very finger tips!' (75:3-4)

قَالُوا۟ يَـٰوَيْلَنَا مَنۢ بَعَثَنَا مِن مَّرْقَدِنَا ۜ ۗ هَـٰذَا مَا وَعَدَ ٱلرَّحْمَـٰنُ وَصَدَقَ ٱلْمُرْسَلُونَ ﴿52﴾

They will say, 'Woe to us! Who raised us from our place of sleep?' 'This is what the All-beneficent had promised, and the apostles had spoken the truth!'

After waking from this long sleep, the feeling of bewilderment and wonder persist, 'They say: Are we indeed restored to our former state in the grave? Even after we were crumbled bones?' (79:10-11) How have we become flesh and bone again? While this new body was being fashioned they were still asleep and unaware, thus they cannot understand where it has appeared from. The body may appear different in many ways yet even its fingerprints are the same as before, 'Does man think that we shall not reassemble his bones? In fact, we are able to restore his very finger tips!' (75:3-4) They are so similar to their forms in this world that they can recognize each other. 'And on the Day that he shall gather them together, it will seem as if they had not tarried except for an hour of the day, and they will recognize one another.' (10:45)

Human beings will emerge like scattered ants from the earth and remain waiting next to their graves. It will take some time for the stupor of their long sleep to dispel. They will be wiping away the dust and grime from their faces as they look around in amazement, unsure about what exactly has happened. They do not know how they have awakened in a new body after just a short sleep. As far as they can see, they are back in their former human form and have come out of the ground and are sitting next to their graves. Their great number resembles moths that flutter in a vast and desolate desert, 'The Day on which mankind will be as scattered moths.' (101:4) It is at this juncture that the faithless see themselves at great loss and say 'woe to us!'

They will say, 'Woe to us!'; This is a statement made by the faithless only, those who used to deny the Resurrection and now suddenly they see themselves resurrected. The first question they ask is "who raised us from our place of sleep?" The word they are quoted to use here is *marqad* from *ruqūd* which means sleep.

Most probably, this does not refer to their lives in *barzakh* as they were wakeful there. It therefore refers to that state of limbo between the two blows of the trumpet in which all souls are unconscious.

'Who raised us from our place of sleep?'; They are still blinded by their disbelief not recognising the power of God and that it is only he who can give life and take life. They are still in their old ignorance of seeing power in hands of agents other than God, which is why they are bewildered as to who has raised them from their slumber.

'This is what the All-beneficent had promised, and the apostles had spoken the truth!' This is either a redress statement by them realising the truth, or a statement by the believers bringing them out of their ignorance. If the former, then it is a confession to what they used to deny in the world and an acknowledgment of God as *al-Raḥmān,* and veracity of his messengers. If the latter, it implies that they are now guided by the believers to the truth. In both cases, they are enlightened about the situation that they are in now.

> إِن كَانَتْ إِلَّا صَيْحَةً وَاحِدَةً فَإِذَا هُمْ جَمِيعٌ لَّدَيْنَا مُحْضَرُونَ ﴿53﴾
>
> It will be but a single Cry, and, behold, they will all be presented before Us!

Humankind will be presented finally, before Allah. That is the encounter (*liqā'*) which will eventually come. 'O man! You are labouring toward your Lord laboriously, and you will encounter him.' (84:5) That is the destination of our journey and the prime moment of our eternal existence.

The verse alludes to the fact that raising the dead in their multitudes is easy for God and takes not more than a single blast. It also implies that the world of *ākhirah* is a world of presence before God. That is a stage where the evolution of the creation as a whole would come to its completion. 'To God belongs the kingdom of the heavens and the earth, and toward God is the destination.' (24:42) 'We belong to God and to him do we return.' (2:156) His presence is felt everywhere and in everything, unlike this world in which people of weak or no faith feel he is hidden behind the chain of the causes and effects.

> فَٱلْيَوْمَ لَا تُظْلَمُ نَفْسٌ شَيْئًا وَلَا تُجْزَوْنَ إِلَّا مَا كُنتُمْ تَعْمَلُونَ ﴿54﴾
>
> 'Today no soul will be wronged in the least, nor will you be requited except for what you used to do.'

'Today no soul will be wronged in the least'; There are many verses in the Qur'ān which deny any *dhulm* or injustice on the Day of Judgement. This emphasis might be due to the enormity of punishment, or more accurately, the consequential ordeal which awaits the wrongdoers. The trial and suffering will be so great and excruciating that one may think it is not just compared to the very short life in this world. The length of the stay and the enormity of the consequences make one think that the requital is not just. That is probably why Allah stresses time and again that no injustice is done on that day. In other words, what is defined as the agonising state of the wrongdoers is just a description of a systematic and consequential outcome of their actions and attitudes, not something that Allah would conventionally punish them with; this is explained by the following sentence in the verse.

'...nor will you be requited except for what you used to do'; The same deeds will be incarnated and find existential forms and will be with us in all stations on the Resurrection day, and after the reckoning is completed, they will be with us as our companions. In this sense, injustice is impossible. It is simply the deliverance of the fruits of one's deeds. In fact, injustice in such a system has no meaning at all. If injustice is possible in this world, it is because recompense is conventional, or because there are human desires or errors involved in the judgement, or because it is not possible to gauge and balance the enormity of the deed with the size of the punishment. However, none of these are possible on that day since it is the deeds themselves that are delivered back to people. In fact, this is not something that Allah has brought upon us. It is something that our actions have brought upon ourselves. This is after the removal of everything that can be forgiven and only those who are not able to receive the mercy of God see those consequences.

Forgiveness of Allah will include all people as long as it does not disrupt the balance and stability of the creation. If Allah forgives someone who would continue to cause harm to himself and others after being forgiven, then the whole idea of Paradise would be inadequate. For either Allah should take their free will before letting them in Paradise in which case it is not Paradise anymore; or he should let them do whatever they want there, in which case nothing comes out of their evil soul but evil, while evil is not permissible in Paradise.

So, in the other world there will be reward and punishment but it is not at all conventional. It is the real repercussion of what we have done; it is our personality which unfolds there into a new form and that is our reward or punishment. Hence, 'today no soul will be wronged in the least.'

Here is a more tangible example. If a state legislates a law that anyone passing a red light must be executed, we may question the justice of such legislation. It is obvious that the punishment is not in proportion with the crime. It is an unjust convention to set such a harsh punishment for such a small crime. However, if by passing a red light an accident occurs and the trespasser is killed, no one would say that it was not just. This is because it was not a legal convention but a real repercussion. That is how things are going to be in the Hereafter. 'There every soul will examine what it has sent in advance' (10:30), and therefore there is no *dhulm*.

Apparently, this system of justice works in this world as well without us realising it. Every wrongdoing has a repercussion in this world and every good act has a real reward attached to it. For example, giving charity with the right intention may bring us more *rizq*, health in our body and blessings in our life that may not be recognised as the result of that charity. On the other hand, wronging someone may bring insurmountable complications to our life without us realising where it has come from. The system is in place here but it goes unnoticed. However, in the Hereafter, this system is all apparent and ostensibly recognizable. It comes to its completion.

We can also take the example of *ṣalāt*. If *ṣalāt* is performed correctly and with the required humbleness and presence of the heart, it would enhance our spirituality and our awareness of God. It would open the eyes of the heart to the extent that one can feel the presence of God around. We may obtain these feelings and that awareness without realising that they are the consequences of our *ṣalāt*. However, in the world of *ākhirah*, the relation between acts and their consequences becomes clear. Moreover, one can see that their *ṣalāt* is actually incarnated into a pleasurable reward. They can experience it. This is the meaning of 'There every soul will examine what it has sent in advance' (10:30) If this is the case no *dhulm* can ever take place there. 'Today every soul shall be given what it has earned. There will be no injustice today. Indeed, Allah is swift at reckoning.' (40:17)

That is why the Qur'ān never quotes the people of Hell complaining of injustice. They express their misery and their agony and they beseech God to release them from their misfortune, but they do not see what is falling on them as injustice; they never say we did not deserve this. 'They will say, "Our Lord! Our wretchedness overcame us, and we were an astray lot. Our Lord! Bring us out of this! Then, if we revert, we will indeed be wrongdoers."' (23:106-107) They realise that this is what they have created for themselves. 'Indeed, Allah does not wrong people in the least; rather it is people who wrong themselves.'(10:44)

That is why the Qur'ān talks about the book of actions, not the book of judgment:

> The Book will be set up. Then you will see the guilty apprehensive of what is in it. They will say, "Woe to us! What a book is this! It omits nothing, big or small, without enumerating it." They will find present whatever they had done, and your Lord does not wrong anyone. (18:49)

They find their actions there. Not the reward or punishment of their actions, but their very actions themselves. It is the actions which are returned and they are the means of recompense. All the actions in a person's life are presented in one time and place. Our personality changes over time during our lives. Sometimes we are good, sometimes we are bad; sometimes our personality persistently continues with a type of quality and that quality becomes a part of our personality and at other times we might lose that aspect and become a completely different person. So, when the actions are put together on the Day of Judgment, an overall personality is shaped; and that personality is the real us. A personality which now incarnates as us; a new person who is nothing but those actions which each has done.

إِنَّ أَصْحَٰبَ ٱلْجَنَّةِ ٱلْيَوْمَ فِى شُغُلٍ فَٰكِهُونَ ﴿55﴾

Indeed today the inhabitants of Paradise rejoice in their engagements

This verse and the following three verses are mentioned in parenthesis in the midst of the discussion about the calamity befalling the people of Hell. The previous verses talked about how the wrongdoers are going to be taken into account, how they react to the event of Resurrection, and how they are going to be dealt with. These verses about the people of Paradise are mentioned to provide a comparison between the wrongdoers and the good doers. People who have done well in this world are in ease and in comfort in the other world.

The term 'inhabitants of Paradise,' *aṣḥāb al-jannah*, is usually used in the Qur'ān to refer to those who have done good in this world and are consequently accommodated in *Jannah*. This is a very broad term which encompasses the most excellent believers like the prophets and the Imams, as well as those who have entered the Paradise after forgiveness and intercession have saved them. Paradise is comprised of different compartments, levels and degrees. Hell is the same too. 'Observe how we have given some of them preference over some others; yet the Hereafter is surely greater in respect of ranks and greater in respect of relative merit.' (17:21)

The term 'day' in the Qur'ān is used in two ways. One is the duration between the dawn to sunset, and the other is any duration of time. For example, when a verse talks about the creation of heavens and earth in six days, it means six periods or phases. So, the Day of Judgement and the Day of Resurrection, refer to that period of our life which has not come yet. It does not mean a day as opposed to night, since it might include many nights as well.

On that day, the people of Paradise are completely occupied by their own lofty engagements. They are not aware of the fate of the people of Hell and the suffering that they endure. They are busy with the bounties of Allah and are cleansed from all agonies and pains, enjoying the utmost joy and pleasure.

The term *fākih*, translated here as 'joyful' has two

meanings. One is a humorous person, someone who is joyous and is good humoured, and the other is someone who is experiencing pleasure and is rejoicing. Although the people of Paradise are engaged in functions, these functions and occupations are full of pleasure. The term *shughul*, 'engagements,' is used in the indefinite form to imply that it is impossible for us to know what type of engagements people would have in Paradise. Our conceptual tools are short of understanding the type and the purpose of life in Paradise.

The only thing we may know is that the people of Paradise have two types of pleasing engagements. One is the physical engagement having their own lives in their palaces, enjoying the company of their spouses and family and partaking from whatever is provided for them by their Lord, and the other is their spiritual engagement experiencing new and fresh manifestations of Allah at each moment. They also have social occasions when they come together in regal gatherings talking and socializing. 'On brocaded couches reclining on them, face to face. They will be waited upon by immortal youths, with goblets and pitchers and a cup of a clear wine, which neither causes them headache nor stupefaction.' (56:15-19)

It is difficult to speculate about the purpose of these gatherings and the content of their speech when they gather. They may share their unique experiences with their Lord. Each person has a different experience of God both in this world and in Paradise because God is infinite and each one of us is just like a conduit; like a container which can contain the knowledge of God according to its own shape and capacity. When the experience of Allah comes inside any one of us, it takes a shape which is different from anyone else's experiences. When people of Paradise talk to each other about this, they rejoice when they learn about different aspects and manifestations of God.

The huge diversity that we see in this world among human beings; the colourful favours of Allah that he bestows differently on people; the unique psychology, attitude, feelings and comprehension of each individual in this world would continue to exist in Paradise. That would make every person unique in their experience of God and this could joyfully be shared with others. This is only a speculation, because the purpose and meaning of each stage of our life only comes with it and cannot be known before it.

هُم وَأَزْوَاجُهُم فِي ظِلَلٍ عَلَى ٱلْأَرَآئِكِ مُتَّكِـُٔونَ ﴿56﴾

—they and their mates, reclining on couches in the shades.

Azwāj (singular. *zawj*) is translated here as *mates*. However, *zawj* has two meanings. One meaning is 'spouse', and the other meaning is 'type'. Both meanings have been used in the Qur'ān. For example, in the verse 'Muster the wrongdoers and their types (*azwājahum*) and what they used to worship besides Allah, and show them the way to Hell!' (37:22-23) *Zawj* is used in the second meaning. Both meanings are possible in this verse although majority of the exegetes have interpreted it as 'spouses.'

The 'shades' may refer to the shades of the trees in Paradise amidst which the 'raised couches' are erected. Or it may refer to the shades of the canopies set for them in the garden of their palaces under which the tables are set. It indicates that the sky is illuminated in Paradise which makes life more pleasurable for its inhabitants.

It may also mean that the whole climate in Paradise feels like being in shade all the time. This may be understood from the phrase *dhillin mamdūd* in Surah al-Wāqi'ah. 'And the People of the Right Hand what are the People of the Right Hand?

Amid thornless lote trees, and clustered spathes, and extended shade.' (56: 27-30)

Arā'ik (sl. *Arīkah*) usually refers to decorated

couches. It is used to express the luxurious life in Paradise. The food, the cutlery, the clothing, the ornaments, the couches, the palaces, the colours, the material, all reveal that sense of luxury in the reader:

> They will be served around with vessels of silver and goblets of crystal. Crystal of silver from which they dispense in a precise measure. They will be served therein with a cup of a drink seasoned with *Zanjabil*, a spring in it, named *Salsabil*. They will be waited upon by immortal youths, whom, when you see them, you will suppose them to be scattered pearls. As you look, you will see there bliss and a great kingdom. Upon them will be cloaks of green silk and brocade and they will be adorned with bracelets of silver. Their Lord will give them to drink a pure drink. (76:15-21)

لَهُمْ فِيهَا فَاكِهَةٌ وَلَهُم مَّا يَدَّعُونَ ﴿57﴾

There they have fruits, and they have whatever they want.

There they have fruits; fruits (*fākihatun*), is used in the indefinite form which signifies our lack of comprehension of the type of fruits in that realm. It is called fruit there, but it is not necessarily similar to what we call fruit here. It also may have wider meaning in terms of the fruits of one's actions performed in this world that they receive there every moment. It is the realisation of the verse in Surah Ibrāhīm:

> Have you not regarded how Allah has drawn a parable? A good word is like a good tree: its roots are steady and its branches are in the sky. It gives its fruit every so often by the leave of its Lord. Allah draws these parables for mankind so that they may take admonition. (14:24-25)

And they have whatever they want; This is a very compelling statement. It tells us that demand and aspiration never cease in humankind. It is one of the signs of the infinite nature of Allah. Despite having everything at our disposal, there are still demands and aspirations which are yet to be fulfilled. The fact that our aspirations are infinite is a sign that there is an infinite being who has placed such an infinite desire in our system.

This demand, despite the satisfaction of all our needs, comes from the unending growth in Paradise. Whatever we shall see in Paradise will be a representation of our inner state; and because that state will be continually evolving, as we grow wiser and love God more deeply, we demand more; and more is given to us. That is why Paradise itself will also continue to evolve. The nature, colour and fragrance of everything in Paradise will constantly improve and become more wondrous. The meaning of time in Paradise arises from this very evolution within us.

Wisdom and love have always been embedded in every human being because it is through these faculties that man's eternal soul – which God placed within the human being – is connected to him. In Paradise man explores his soul every day and removes the veils that mask the beauty of that wisdom and love so that he can see himself more clearly, or rather see God more clearly; it does not make a difference in fact, because his ego does not exist anymore. What he sees now is his true self, which is one with his cognitive soul; and so, he will see and know God to the same degree as he knows himself. He will be a mirror that reflects the beauty of God. Whatever he sees inside himself is manifested externally too.

It is similar to the names of God when they manifest themselves in the physical realm, or possibly the names of God manifesting themselves through them in the outside world. Therefore, with the removal of every inner veil, the flowers and gardens he sees externally are transformed as well. The appearance and decorations of his palaces and the elegance of his garments all take on a new beauty because his new growth demands it.

> سَلَٰمٌ قَوْلًا مِّن رَّبٍّ رَّحِيمٍ ﴿58﴾
>
> 'Peace!'—a watchword from the all-merciful Lord.

All those bounties and pleasures are amplified when a constant peace is imbued in them by the merciful Lord. It should be born in mind that as the substance of physical elements like gold, silver, pearls, and rubies in Paradise descends from the *malakūt*, they are different in nature from what we know of them here. Similarly, the very nature of mental elements like peace, contentment, and love therein would be different from what we know of them in this world. For example, peace in this world could only be defined negatively as the absence of disturbance, while peace in Paradise is a positive existential thing which we yet have to experience.

Some exegetes say that this verse is, in fact, an explanation for 'what they demand.' They demand this peace and greeting from their merciful Lord which is above all their enjoyments in Paradise. This is what they really aspire for, because all other enjoyments of Paradise are dwarfed in comparison. This refreshing and pleasant *salām*, which is full of his love and affection, attracts them so deeply, and gives them such an enlivening spiritual joy that it does not match any other bounty. This peace is so prevalent in Paradise that Allah calls it the abode of peace. 'Allah invites to the abode of peace, and he guides whomever he wishes to a straight path.' (10:25)

وَٱمْتَـٰزُواْ ٱلْيَومَ أَيُّهَا ٱلْمُجْرِمُونَ ﴿59﴾

And 'Get apart today, you guilty ones!'

All those blessings mentioned; peace, fruits of actions, and fulfilment of demands and desires, are for those who do not have *dhulm* (injustice) on their hands or crimes on their record. Those with such a record have to 'get apart' from *ashāb al-jannah*. For them there will be darkness and disappointment. 'The day the Trumpet will be blown on that day we shall muster the guilty with blind eyes.' (20:102) and 'he will fail who bears the onus of wrongdoing.' (20:111)

The separation of the good and evil on that day is according to the justice and wisdom of God. 'So that Allah may separate the evil from the good, and place the evil ones on one another, and pile them up together, and cast them into Hell. It is they who are the losers.' (8:37) It is the realization of the eternal destiny God has disposed for good and evil. 'Shall we treat those who have faith and do righteous deeds like those who cause corruption on the earth? Shall we treat the God wary like the vicious?' (38:28)

However, although the apparent meaning of the verse refers to the separation of the guilty from the faithful, some early commentators, such as the *tābi'ī* scholar al-Zaḥḥāk, have inclined to the meaning of separation of the guilty from each other, each group going towards a different destination. Even more dramatically, he claims that not only are each type of criminal separated from each other, but also every individual criminal and disbeliever will be separated from others and locked in a solitary confinement until eternity. It is, however, difficult to accept this understanding within the context of this verse.

Good and evil part ways in the *ākhirah*, but opinions differ about the time and length of this separation. The mainstream opinion is that as we all live alongside each other in this world, we will continue to do so after we die. Similarly, we will all be together when we are resurrected, as many verses of the Qur'ān allude. 'They will be placed within each other's sight. The guilty one will wish he could ransom himself from the punishment of that day at the price of his children.' (70:11) Then, at one station on the Day of Resurrection the existential command of separation occurs. This is something that God causes to occur naturally and not through a conventional command. It is because of this complete parting of ways that the Resurrection Day is called *yawm al-faṣl*, the Day of Separation.

On reflection, there is a degree of separation in this world too. This is related to the type of inner world in which every person lives. This is clearly alluded to in the verse of Surah Jāthīyah, 'Do those who have perpetrated misdeeds suppose that we shall treat them as those who have faith and do righteous deeds, their life and death being equal? Evil is the judgement that they make.' (45:21) Here Allah informs us that lives in this world are not equal. This is likely to be an allusion to the pure life (*al-ḥayāt al-Ṭayyebah*) that Allah gives to the exceptional believers in this world. 'Whoever acts righteously, whether male or female, should he be faithful, we shall revive him with a pure life and pay them their reward by the best of what they used to do.' (16:97)

The 'pure life' is a life which is not adulterated by the deception of this world. It is a life in which God is present and visible by the heart of the believer. It is in this way that those with remarkable faith are separated from the disbelievers. They have a 'pure life' which is not contaminated by ignorance, negligence, arrogance, self-complacency and above all, greed. This is why when Imam Ali (a) was asked about the nature of this pure life, he said, it is 'contentment' (*qanāʾah*). One may say that although contentment is a very good quality, it would not be the distinguishing factor between a believer and a disbeliever.

However, real contentment, the absolute contentment with whatever happens in this world is not possible unless one has a deep knowledge and trust in the creator. These special believers do not question what they are given, rather they question their ability to thank the one who gives. They wake up each morning wondering how best they can remember God; 'Their sides vacate their beds to supplicate their Lord in fear and hope,' (32:16), and they go to bed every evening thoughtful of how best they can thank their Lord. This is how they are distinguished from others. Their values, their aspirations, and what they regard important are different from other people, be they ordinary believers or disbelievers.

أَلَمْ أَعْهَدْ إِلَيْكُمْ يَـٰبَنِىٓ ءَادَمَ أَن لَّا تَعْبُدُوا۟ ٱلشَّيْطَـٰنَ إِنَّهُۥ لَكُمْ عَدُوٌّ مُّبِينٌ ﴿60﴾

'Did I not exhort you, O children of Adam, saying, "Do not worship Satan. He is indeed your manifest enemy.

Did I not exhort you; the word used for exhort in the verse is '*ahd*. '*Ahida ilayhi* can mean 'he exhorted him or advised him' or it can mean 'he took a pledge or covenant from him.' Most commentators have understood the verse as it is translated here: 'Did I not exhort you?' The command of Allah in this regard has reached the children of Adam through his messengers.

Some have postulated that *'ahd* could mean pledge; so, the meaning would be 'Did I not take a pledge from you?' They say the verse talks about the pledge taken from Adam in the 'world of particles' (*ālam al-dhar*) alluded to in Surah A'arāf:

> When your Lord took from the Children of Adam, from their loins, their descendants and made them bear witness over themselves, [he said to them,] "Am I not your Lord?" They said, "Yes indeed! We bear witness." This, lest you should say on the Day of Resurrection, "Indeed we were unaware of this." (7:172)

However, this meaning is not intended here. Firstly, because the pledge of *ālam al-dhar*, according the verse, is not about worship but the Lordship (*rubūbīyyah*) of God. It says nothing about worshipping him and not worshipping Satan. Secondly, the commentators and the theologians are not in agreement about the concept of *ālam al-dhar* and adopting this meaning would result in many unanswered questions.

O children of Adam; As some commentators have said, humankind is addressed here as *children of Adam* to remind them of the plight of their forefather Adam when he obeyed Satan. This is similar to the advice given to us in Surah A'rāf in which after recounting the story of Adam and Eve, Allah advises us as children of Adam; 'O Children of Adam! Do not let Satan tempt you, like he expelled your parents from Paradise, stripping them of their garments to expose to them their nakedness.' (7:27)

Do not worship Satan; The essence of worship is two things, to humble one's self to someone and to obey them. The main pillar of worship is obedience. If we do not obey God, we are certainly not worshipping him. So here worshipping Satan means obeying him in humility, which is translated in action as following one's desires outside the boundaries defined by God. It is reported from Imam Ja'far as Ṣādiq (a) that 'Whoever obeys a person in disobedience of God has worshipped him.' And it is recorded from Imam al-Baqir (a) that 'Whoever listens to and follows a speaker, has worshipped him. If the speaker speaks from Allah, he has worshipped Allah, and if the speaker speaks from Satan, he has worshipped Satan.'

He is indeed your manifest enemy; Satan is a 'manifest enemy' though we cannot see him. This is because he is an enemy who has manifested his animosity towards humankind. 'Manifest enemy' is an enemy who does not conceal his animosity. Satan has manifested his animosity towards the children of Adam from the outset. 'He said, "By Your might, I will surely seduce them all."' (38:82) And 'Said he, "Do you see this one whom you have honoured above me? If you respite me until the Day of Resurrection, I will surely destroy his progeny all, except a few."' (17:62) So, he is clearly an outspoken enemy of man. He has not concealed his hatred, rather he has declared it openly.

A Note about Satan

There are many questions that arise when discussing the issue of Satan: Is Satan a real being or is it a metaphorical name for the evil whispers of the soul? Is it a concept or a person? When Allah talks about Shaytān coming and deceiving us, is he really talking about someone coming to us, telling us things, and we obey him and worship him, or is this a metaphor used for our ill desires and wrong doings?

If we say he is a real creature, we might question how he can be so powerful and omnipresent, such that he can influence many people around the world simultaneously. The Qur'ān tells us that he is in fact a time-bound creature when he asked for respite *until* the Day of Judgement, and Allah gave him respite until an appointed time. 'He said, "My Lord! Respite me till the day they will be resurrected." Said he, "You are indeed among the reprieved until the day of the known time."' (38:79-81)

The Qur'ān unequivocally states that Iblīs is a real figure from the *jinn*, under whom many other evil *jinn* (*Shaytān*) work.

So *Shaytān* is an attribute for Iblīs and his accomplices from *jinn* who have the power to interfere with our desires and imagination without us realizing it. 'Indeed, he sees you, he and his hosts from where you do not see them' (7:27) Iblīs was one of the *jinn* who was raised to the rank of angels then failed to obey the orders of God. 'He was one of the *jinn*, so he transgressed against his Lord's command. Will you then take him and his offspring for guardians in my stead, though they are your enemies?' (18:50)

Overlooking the apparent meaning of all the verses which speak of Iblīs in this way in order to pursue the idea that he is simply metaphorical would be an illogical method of understanding. It is not right hermeneutically to give meaning to a small part of a text which would then require deviating from the apparent meaning in all other parts of the text. In this case, arguing that Satan is a figurative term, would mean deviating from the apparent meaning of quite a large number of verses.

Here it is important to understand the nature if *jinn*. Again, they are not figurative creatures; rather they are intelligent beings like humans who have free will, life and death, resurrection, judgment and Heaven and Hell. They, like us, live on this earth, although in a different dimension. That is why we usually do not see them although they see us. Their dimension allows them access to us while we do not have access to them. They are like many other creatures that our senses cannot perceive.

In the same way that we are created from clay, *jinn* are created from fire. 'He created man out of dry clay, like the potter's, and created the *jinn* out of a flame of a fire.' (55:14-15) That does not mean that they look like fire now, but the origin of their body's matter is fire as the origin of our body's matter is dust. They have evolved out of fire as we have evolved out of dust. We can understand what this evolution means in our own case, because everything that nourishes us as embryos and as born human beings come from dust. In the same way, we can speculate that everything that nourishes *jinn* as embryos and as born *jinn* comes from gas and fire. Being created from fire does not mean that they like fire or they are not hurt by fire. We are created from dust and clay, but we hate dust, we do not like to sit on dust, and we cannot eat dust. We die if we are buried under the dust, and bricks and rocks made of out of dust can harm us.

As far as we can understand from the Qur'ān, the *jinn* have limited spiritual capacity compared to humans. They do not receive scriptures from God, and they follow the scriptures revealed to human beings. They may have prophets of their own but their prophets do not receive revelations from God; they go to human prophets, receive the word, understand it, accept it, and then convey it to their people. This is why they have the same religions as we do. There may be Christian or Jewish or Muslim *jinn*. Through the guidance of these religions they may attain high positions with God. They can become *awlīyāʾAllāh* (friends of Allah) as we understand from Surah Jinn.

The few verses that we have in the Qur'an about *jinn* reveal a good amount of information about them. For example, in Surah Jinn they are quoted saying, 'Among us some are righteous and some of us are otherwise: we are multifarious sects.' (72:11) This righteousness is probably of the rank mentioned about Prophet Lūt (a); 'And we admitted him into our mercy. Indeed, he was one of the righteous.' (21:75), which is the caliber of *awlīyāʾAllāh*. These multifarious sects are different classes of believer *jinn*s; like us they have *jinn* with very high faith and *jinn* with lower faith grades. However they have vicious groups as well. 'Among us some are Muslims and some of us are perverse. Yet those who submit it is they who pursue rectitude. As for the perverse, they will be firewood for Hell.' (72:14-15)

The Qur'ān talks about *jinn* in details in two surahs,

Surah Aḥqāf and Surah Jinn. The *jinn* in Surah Aḥqāf are apparently followers of the Scripture of Moses. 'When we dispatched toward you a team of *jinn* listening to the Qur'an, when they were in its presence, they said, "Be silent!" When it was finished, they went back to their people as warners.' (46:29)

This group of *jinn* who were directed towards the Prophet (s) were apparently those *awliyā'Allāh* among *jinn*. They were to become prophets of their communities. After learning the Qur'ān, they went back to their community and said, 'O our people! Indeed, we have heard a Book which has been sent down after Moses, confirming what was before it. It guides to the truth and to a straight path.' (46:30) So, they were following the Book of Moses, and after they heard the Qur'ān and understood it, they testified that it guides to the truth and to a straight path. These were the Prophets of *jinn* who went back to their community as warners. 'O our people! Respond to Allah's summoner and have faith in him. He will forgive you some of your sins and shelter you from a painful punishment.' (46:31)

The *jinn* mentioned in Surah Jinn are different. They believed that God had a son. They have been quoted as saying, 'Exalted be the majesty of our Lord, he has taken neither any spouse nor son. Indeed, the foolish ones among us used to utter atrocious lies concerning Allah.' (72:3-4) Their encounter with the Prophet (s) probably happened in a mosque in Makkah which was later called *Masjid al-Jinn*. A group of them came when the Prophet (s) was reciting the Qur'ān in his night prayer, and soon they increased in number to the extent that when the Prophet (s) stood up to perform the morning prayer, the mosque was overflowing with *jinn*. 'When the servant of Allah rose to pray to him, they almost crowded him (to death).' (72: 19) The suggestion of the verses is that the Prophet (s) was not aware of their presence until Allah revealed it to him. 'Say, It has been revealed to me that a team of the *jinn* listened to the Qur'an, and they said, "Indeed, we heard a wonderful Qur'an."' (72:1)

Thus, in terms of guidance, they are closely following what has been revealed to human prophets. They know more about us and our Imams and Messengers than we know about them. The reason for their existence in this world is exactly like ours, that is, to be perfected for Paradise. 'Those who submit' among the *jinn* 'it is they who pursue rectitude and perfection.' The perverse among them are going to be firewood of Hell as it is said about the perverse among the human. 'Indeed, you and what you worship besides Allah shall be fuel for Hell.' (21:98)

How does Satan work in our hearts and minds?

Satan cannot come to all of us at once or to allocate a slot of time to every one of us. So, to spread his mischief, he needs accomplices to work as his army. This is alluded to in Surah Isrā' after Iblīs challenges Allah for giving Adam such a high position.

> When we said to the angels, "Prostrate before Adam," they all prostrated, but not Iblīs: he said, "Shall I prostrate before someone whom you have created from clay?" Then he said, "Do you see this one whom you have honoured above me? If you respite me until the Day of Resurrection, I will surely destroy his progeny, all except a few." (17:61-62)

In other words, Iblīs challenged the wisdom of God by arguing that Adam was not superior to him, and that if he could be given respite, he would prove this. Allah said:

> Begone! Whoever of them follows you, indeed the Hell shall be your requital, an ample reward. Instigate whomever of them you can with your voice; and rally against them your cavalry and your infantry, and share with them in wealth and children, and make promises to them! But

Satan promises them nothing but delusion.' (17:63-64)

It is important to know that Satan has no power over anyone except for the power of deception, it is just a voice in the heart and mind; and if that voice is not listened to, he is abjectly defeated. That is why the Qur'ān says, 'Indeed, the stratagems of Satan are always flimsy.' (4:76)

Secondly, he has foot soldiers and cavalry. This means that he does not usually come to us himself, he sends his soldiers to us. The foot soldiers of Satan are in fact humans. We are his foot soldiers, we go to each other, and call each other to wrong causes. His cavalry are the evil *jinn*, the *shayātīn* who are from his own kind. They come and attack us in our mind and heart with aggrandizing our desires and ambitions and fooling us by unachievable aspirations. 'He makes them promises and gives them false hopes, yet Satan does not promise them anything but delusion.' (4:120)

Like some humans who can put thoughts in the mind of others by telepathy, they have a power to interfere with the minds of those who show some propensity towards them. 'Indeed, he sees you he and his hosts whence you do not see them. We have indeed made the devils friends of those who have no faith.' (7:27) That is how we are driven by them, but if we do not give into the imaginational aspirations that they promote in our minds, and instead use the power of reason, all their efforts crumble. However, as soon as we give in to those imaginations, the intellect renders itself ineffective.

A verse in Surah al-Nisā' says 'he makes them promises and gives them false hopes.' An example of these false hopes and promises is mentioned in Surah Baqarah; 'Satan frightens you of poverty and prompts you to commit indecent acts.' (2:268) He gives us false hope and promises by convincing us that through committing indecent acts we can attain our goals. Any time we want to give charity he frightens us with poverty. However, 'Allah promises you his forgiveness and grace.' (2:268) The angels imbue in our mind and heart real hope, and promise us grace from God.

It is not only Satan who is working to influence us, it is the angels of God too. And it is for us to choose who to listen to. On the day when everything becomes transparent, Iblīs will tell us that he did not have any power over us but the power of invitation and promise:

> When the matter is all over, Satan will say, "Indeed Allah made you a promise that was true and I too made you a promise, but I failed you. I had no authority over you, except that I called you and you responded to me. So, do not blame

me, but blame yourselves. I cannot respond to your distress calls, neither can you respond to my distress calls." (14:22)

There are two verses in the Qur'ān that specifically talk about how the evil *jinn* (*shayāṭīn*) find their way to our mind and heart and manipulate our thoughts and imaginations. The first is the verses in Surah al-Zukhruf:

> Whoever turns a blind eye to the remembrance of the All-beneficent, we assign him a devil who remains his companion. And they bar them from the way while they suppose that they are rightly guided. When he comes to us, he will say, "I wish there had been between me and you the distance between east and west! What an evil companion are you." (43:36-39)

The people who follow these assigned companies think that they are enlightened intellectuals who know more than others. They regard other people as lay and illiterate who are backward and lack acumen and understanding. This is what the people of Prophet Nūḥ (a) told him, 'We do not see anyone following you except those who are simple-minded riff-raff from our midst. Nor do we see that you have any merit over us. Rather we consider you to be liars.' (11:27)

The other verse talks about the way the evil *jinn* carry out their function. 'We assigned for them companions who would make their past and present [deeds] seem attractive to them. Thus, they became subject to what the *jinn* and human beings before were destined to suffer. They were certainly lost.' (41:25) The evil *jinn*'s function is to embellish evil and make Godly values seem unimportant. The future unwarranted ambitions and the people who are accompanied by them as well as the evil actions of their past would all be made to seem to them as good.

When the devils find us as potential listeners to their whispers and start accompanying us, it is difficult to get rid of them. Prophet Ibrahim (a) told his stepfather, Āzar, 'Father! I am indeed afraid that a punishment from the All-beneficent will befall you, and you will become Satan's accomplice.' (19:45) It is the consequence of ignoring the signs of God which attracts these devils and here it is referred to as the punishment of God. Another verse in the same surah talks of dispatching the *shayātin* to the disbelievers to bring about evil urges in them. 'Have you not regarded that we unleash the devils upon the faithless to urge them impetuously.' (19:83)

Finally, when a devil becomes a companion to a person and the individual does not try to get rid of it, then they both go to the judgment together and both will be sent to Hell together. They will argue with each other in the presence of God regarding their guilt each trying to put the blame on the other:

> His satanic companion will say, "Our Lord, I did not mislead him, but he himself went astray". The Lord will say, "Do not argue in my presence; I had certainly sent you a warning. No word is to be exchanged in my presence. I am not unjust to my servants." (50:27-29)

وَأَنِ ٱعْبُدُونِى هَـٰذَا صِرَاطٌ مُّسْتَقِيمٌ ﴿61﴾

Worship Me. That is a straight path"?

Worship Me; Human beings are worshipping creatures even if the objects of worship are themselves. Allah does not allow us to worship Satan, and he does not want us to worship anything less than him because it is worthless and transitory. What Allah has destined for us is nothing less than the highest excellence that is worshipping him and nothing less than him. This is what he explicitly mentions in Surah al-Dhārīyāt; 'I did not create the *jinn* and the humans except that they may worship me. I desire no provision from them, nor do I desire that they should feed me.' (51:56-57)

That is a straight path; The very concept of 'path' (*ṣirāt*) indicates a journey and a destination. It implies that this life is not a resting place but a journey towards somewhere else and a path to something higher. The path which takes us directly to that destination is 'worship of God.' This worship cannot be mixed with any obedience to Satan which is tantamount to disobedience of God. The verse implies that apart from this straight path there are other paths which may lead to the same destination but they are not straight. The straight path is the shortest path between two points. The paths which are not straight may also take us to him but with a longer distance and with much more difficulty. This is the path of those who pollute worship of God with sins and disobedience.

وَلَقَدْ أَضَلَّ مِنكُمْ جِبِلًّا كَثِيرًا أَفَلَمْ تَكُونُوا۟ تَعْقِلُونَ ﴿62﴾

Certainly, he has led astray many of your generations. Have you not exercised your reason?

After reminding us of his command and covenant that we should not worship Satan, this verse informs us of a historical fact. 'Certainly, he has led astray many of your generations.' Reflecting on past nations, we see how many miseries Satan has brought upon his followers. What painful and evil fate he wrought upon his followers among the ancient civilizations. The ruins of their cities are a clear caution for future generations.

In the commentary on this verse Sheikh Ṭūsī and Sheikh Ṭabrasī believe that this verse refutes the claim of pre-determinists (*Mujabbirah*) that it is God who misguides people. If Allah has a determined will for some people to be misguided then that is even more damaging than the effort of Satan to misguide them. And if he does so, how can he say that Satan has misguided many multitudes of you? Sheikh Ṭūsī then attempts to tackle a verse which seems contrary to his conclusion. 'Indeed, Allah leads astray whomever he wishes, and guides whomever he wishes.' (35:8) He says that turning the faithless astray from the path of Paradise or passing a ruling on the faithless to go astray is something desirable, unlike the misguidance of Satan which is vexatious. It is only after they welcome the misguidance of Satan that Allah passes that ruling on them and separates them from believers.

Reflecting on the three verses which contain the above objectionable meaning shows that Sheikh Ṭūsī's view is enlightened. In Sura al-Raʿd we read, 'The faithless say, "Why has not some sign been sent down to him from his Lord?" Say, "Indeed Allah leads astray whomever he wishes, and guides to himself those who turn penitently to him."' (13:27) Here misguidance is due to their faithlessness which has already come from Satan. Otherwise every penitent soul is guided towards him. In Surah al-Naḥl it is said, 'Had Allah wished, he would have made you one community, but he leads astray whomever he wishes and guides whomever he wishes, and you will surely be questioned concerning what you used to do.' (16:93) This verse clearly indicates that the misguidance here is due to their evil actions. In other words, anyone who is led astray by Satan and perpetrates evil is left by Allah to pursue the wrong direction.

The final verse is in Surah Fāṭir which is partially quoted above; 'Is someone the evil of whose conduct is presented as decorous to him, so he regards it as good [...] Indeed, Allah leads astray whomever he wishes, and guides whomever he wishes.' (35:8) Again, it is the embellishment and exaggeration of Satan who leads people astray and Allah has allowed that in his eternal will.

$$\text{هَٰذِهِ جَهَنَّمُ ٱلَّتِي كُنتُمْ تُوعَدُونَ ﴿63﴾}$$

This is the Hell you had been promised!

This is an address to the followers of Satan who disregarded their covenant with God. They are the *mujrimūn* (the guilty) who were told in verse 59 to 'get apart' from the people of Paradise. An eloquent ellipsis is used here again. They are told to get apart, they are judged, they are taken to Hell, and then they are told, 'This is the Hell you had been warned about.' The warning came to them through multitudes of messengers and prophets - *'kuntum tū'adūn'* which means 'you were continuously being warned about it.'

The separation or 'getting apart' of good from evil and innocent from guilty serves a huge purpose. Hell is a place where corruption and impurity is accumulated and then set on fire, and then time is given to see if their owners are thus purified:

> And the disbelievers will be gathered together in Hell, so that God may separate the impure from the pure; he will heap the impure one upon another and consign them all to Hellfire. Indeed, they are the losers. (8:36-37)

This verse is explained in a beautiful parable by Prophet Isā (a) mentioned in the Gospel of Matthew. 13:24-30:

> That which occurs in the dominion of God is the simile of the person who sowed good seed in his field. One night while he was asleep, his enemy came and sowed weeds amongst his

wheat seeds and left. When the wheat sprouted and formed heads, the weeds also appeared. His servants asked, "Do you want us to pull out the weeds?" He replied, "No, do not do that because while you pull out the weeds, you might uproot the wheat at the same time. Wait until the time when both are ready for harvest. At that time, I will tell the harvesters to collect the weeds in bundles and burn them; thereafter, they can bring the wheat in for storage."

Hell is a place of torment that actually stems from God's mercy. With the extraordinary power that human beings acquire in the Hereafter, if the inmates of Hell were not contained in a fiery prison, not a single moment of peace would remain for anyone. One of the blessings that the dwellers of Heaven are constantly thankful for is the peace they experience as a result of the imprisonment of those who have yet to shed the corruption of their souls. If they were left free, they would not hesitate to trouble every other creature.

Therefore, accruing the corrupt souls and imprisoning them in Hell is nothing but an extension of God's mercy on the rest of his servants:

Once again the dominion of Heaven can be explained with the following parable; fishermen cast a net into the water and catch all kinds of fish. Then they pull it to the shore and separate the good fish from the bad. They place the good fish in baskets and throw away the bad. At the end of time this is what will happen also. The angels will come and separate the righteous individuals from the corrupt; they will throw the corrupt into Hell where they will lay weeping and gnashing their teeth.

This parable is mentioned in Gospel of Matthew, 13:47-50. It is apparent that if any of the inmates of Hell abandons his obstinacy and egoism and his existence is no longer a threat to the wellbeing of others, he will leave Hell and enter a life of bliss. The punishments of Hell are all designed to discourage the inmates of Hell from their arrogance. It has been narrated from the Prophet (s) that, "On the Day of Judgement anyone who has testified to the creed "there is no god but Allah" and whose heart contains an atom's weight of virtue will be removed from Hell." As for those whose hearts did not even have an atom's weight of goodness, they would never be able to abandon their arrogance and consequently must remain in Hell for eternity.

It has been reported from an exegete of the Qur'an of the first century named Ḍaḥḥāk that:

I received a narration of the Prophet (s) in

which I had doubt; to resolve this I set off for Madinah. In the mosque of the Prophet (s) I saw that the people were seated in two groups; at the head of each sat an old man relating the traditions of the Prophet (s). I enquired about these two men and was informed that one of them was Abū Saʿīd al-Khudrī and the other was Abū Hurayra. I came to Abū Saʿīd and said that I had received a report from the Prophet (s) which seemed doubtful to me, and for this reason I had come to Madinah to seek its verification. He asked, "What is this report?" I said, "That the Prophet (s) said that, "A group will be brought out of Hell after they have been turned to coal." Abū Saʿīd pointed to his ear and said, "May both my ears turn deaf if I lie! I have heard the Messenger of God (s) say that mankind will be in different groups on the Day of Judgement; some will enter Paradise without accounting, and these will be the prophets. Others will have to give an account of their deeds, and if their good deeds outnumber their evil ones, then they too will be taken to Paradise; and if their good and evil deeds are equal, God shall be merciful to them and forgive them and they will be taken to Paradise; and I or other qualified people shall intercede for some. And if the situation is different from these two, then they will be taken to Hell, where they will be punished to the extent of their evil, and then they will be brought to their Paradise [...] they will be brought to a spring which is named the "spring of life" (*'ayn al-ḥayāt*) and be instructed to wash themselves in this spring. As they enter the spring all the remaining corruption and arrogance will wash away from their bodies; however, on their forehead there shall remain a sign saying, "These are the servants of God whom he has released from the fire of Hell." When the dwellers of Paradise see them they shall say, "These are the people who have been released from their Hells". Then God removes that too.

There is another very important concept in the Qur'ān which is relevant here. When God speaks about *Jahannam*, he says that Hell will be set on fire on the Day of Judgement, 'and when Hell is set ablaze' (81:12); it means that it is there already but not set on fire yet; this is also inferred in the verse 'and the Hell will be brought into view for the perverse' (26:91) It can be understood from this verse that Hell is already inside us, it just needs something to kindle it, to set it alight; and when we go past all those judgements and all those stages, it will be set alight. This does not contradict the idea that we are sent to a place called Hell, there is a place that we have to go to. We will not live in a vacuum on the Day of Judgement or in *Jahannam*, but the experience of *Jahannam* is inside the people and they are set on fire on the Day of Judgement, by the justice of Allah, or by that attribute of him which is purifying and tends to purify everything. It is set alight to burn all the foolishness and filth that has grown inside them. We can see this meaning indicated in other verses too; 'Beware the Fire whose fuel will be humans and stones, prepared for the faithless.' (2:24); or 'Indeed you and what you worship besides Allah shall be fuel for Hell, and you will come to it.' (21:98); or about *jinn*, it says in Surah Jinn, 'As for the perverse, they will be firewood for Hell.' (72:15) The only thing that needs *Jahannam* to be set alight is that last push of Allah to make us see what is inside us.

ٱصْلَوْهَا ٱلْيَوْمَ بِمَا كُنتُمْ تَكْفُرُونَ ﴿64﴾

Enter it today, because of what you used to deny.

Enter it today; *Salā* can mean to enter a place or to accompany something or someone. Tūsī and Ṭabrasī do not take entrance as part of the meaning of this verse; so, the meaning would be: 'accompany it today,' because of your defiance. Ṭabrasī gives it further meaning too, reporting from the Muʿtazilī scholar Abū Muslim Khorāsānī, he says *salā* means *waqūd* (fuel); so, it means 'you turn into its fuel today.'

Because of what you used to deny; 'denying' or 'defying' is a good translation for *kufr*. This shows that the main cause for entering Hell is disbelief which entails all the evils that should be burnt and purified by the fire. Of course, *kufr*, has different levels of meanings; some levels of *kufr* may not necessary lead to Hell, but some other levels would unavoidably lead a person to destruction.

ٱلۡيَوۡمَ نَخۡتِمُ عَلَىٰٓ أَفۡوَٰهِهِمۡ وَتُكَلِّمُنَآ أَيۡدِيهِمۡ وَتَشۡهَدُ أَرۡجُلُهُم بِمَا كَانُوا۟ يَكۡسِبُونَ ﴿65﴾

Today We shall seal their mouths, and their hands shall speak to Us, and their feet shall bear witness concerning what they used to earn.'

Two issues need to be discussed regarding this verse. The first is sealing the mouth and the reason for it, and the second is the testimony of the limbs.

Today, We shall seal their mouths; we know that what we call the Day of Judgment is a long period of time; it may be thousands of years, with several stations and stages. People are given the chance to talk and argue their case in many of those stations. There are witnesses of different ranks who bear witness at different levels; these include the angels, messengers, and books of records. Of course, God is aware of the inner reality of all deeds, so the testimonies of the witnesses in the court of God are not for his information; rather, they are to make individuals aware of the real meaning of their deeds.

However, despite all proofs and evidence, some people may still remain in denial. We cannot realise fully the extent of human freedom and their behaviour based on their personal judgment in that realm. Because of their freedom and personal justification, some people continue lying in the presence of God as they used to do in this world. Lying and denial has become their intrinsic nature. 'On the Day when God will resurrect them all, they will swear to him as they swear to you and they will imagine that they have some standing. Indeed, they are liars!' (58:18). In Surah al-An'ām, God says:

> The Day we gather them all together we shall say to the polytheists, "So where are the associates whom you asserted?" They will have no excuses left but to say, "By Allah! Our Lord, we were never polytheists." See how they lie against their own interests! But that which they forge will disappear from their sight. (6:22-24)

In the final stage, before the people enter Hell, the denying mouths will be sealed and the limbs with which the acts of injustice were done start to speak.

As it is clear from the above verse, this stage is after the judgement is complete and people are sent towards Hell. When these people are brought to the brink of the Hell then the final testimony comes from their limbs. This is the last proof, which convinces them above all previous testimonies that their destiny is in accordance to justice and truth. What a wonderful testimony it is, where its witnesses are the limbs of the perpetrators themselves by which they have committed the crimes.

It is interesting to point out that in Surah al-Nūr the tongue is also mentioned as one of the limbs that testify. 'On the day when witness shall be given against them by their tongues, their hands, and their feet concerning what they used to do.' (24:24) However, it should be noted that the tongue here would testify as an independent agent not as the means of speech of the criminal. The tongue would say things that the owner of the tongue would not want to say. After all, this speech is different from our speech in this world for which we use tongue. It is a type of communication yet unknown to us.

And their hands shall speak to us, and their feet shall bear witness concerning what they used to earn; How could an inanimate object bear witness on the Day of Judgement? Is it real speech or is it just a metaphor used here for a realm in which everything is exposed to God and to people? Reflecting on the wording of the verse, we see that two different terms are used. Speaking with regards to the hands and bearing witness with regards to the feet. It implies that it is not just bearing witness in any form, but it is bearing witness specifically by speaking.

But for things to be able to speak and bear witness they have to be rational and they have to have identity. What is the identity of the hand that is going to speak? What is the identity of the foot which is going to bear witness? Can we say that our hands are rational beings, that our feet are rational beings? To answer this question, we have to consider that the realm of *ākhira* is very different from the realm of *dunyā*.

Before coming to this world, it was unimaginable for the baby in the womb that they could speak, but coming to this world transforms them in a way that their potential for rationality and for speech are actualised. In the same way, the Qur'ān tells us that there is a potentiality in everything for intelligence that would be actualised in the realm of *ākhira*. 'They will say to their skins, "why did you bear witness against us?" They will say, "we were given speech by Allah, who gave speech to all things"' (41:21). God gives everything the power of speech in that realm. The earth will report back everything that took place on it.

'On that day she will relate her chronicles, for her Lord will have inspired her' (99:4-5).

In a sense, we can say that on the Day of Judgment life will be upgraded in every way. Intelligence will become universal and communication will become possible with everything. The verses in Surah Fuṣṣilat shed further light on this:

> The day when the enemies of God are marched out toward the Fire, and they shall be held in check. When they come to it, their hearing will bear witness against them and their sight and their skins concerning what they used to do. They will say to their skins, "Why did you bear witness against us?" They will say, "We were given speech by God, who gave speech to all things. He created you the first time, and to him you are being brought back." (41:19-21)

It is interesting here that the eyes and skin do not only report back to God who has the power to understand them and they have the humility to expose themselves to him, but they speak to the person who owns them as well. The person will speak with his own skin and will receive a reply. The skin will become a rational being which can be addressed and can address others. It will find intelligence to the extent that it can say, 'he created you the first time.' This is great knowledge. It can say 'we were given speech by God, who gave speech to all things.' This is immense comprehension.

The skin cannot understand this unless it evolves into a rational being capable of comprehension. Furthermore, 'their hands will speak to us, and their feet will bear witness to everything they had done.' Just imagine if things with no comprehension or with very limited comprehension will become rational and be able to testify in this manner, where the rational soul of human being would reach.

One final point that needs to be considered in this relation is the humiliation involved in such a testimony. Allah who is *Sattār* (the Concealer) would expose evil doers on that day in such a humiliating manner. Of course, all of us will be exposed to Allah, but not all of us will be humiliated in this way that our skins, hands, ears, eyes and hearts will speak against us. It will be utterly humiliating when one will try to conceal something, yet their limbs speak out against them. One might wonder *why* they are in such a humiliating position.

To understand this, we need to expand on the whole concept of testimony on the Day of Judgment. If God is a witness, and 'Allah suffices as a witness,' (4:79), why do other beings need to speak and testify? If we are completely exposed to him, what is the purpose? The answer is that on that Day the truth manifests itself in everything and everywhere. It may not be for testimony as such, but since everything speaks the truth, it is as if everything is testifying against the rejecters. Yet, despite such a manifestation of truth, the *kuffār* are still in darkness. They still ask their skins the reason for witnessing against them. Their skins which lacked intelligence in this world, now understand God better than them when they say, 'we were given speech by God, who gave speech to all things.'

وَلَوْ نَشَآءُ لَطَمَسْنَا عَلَىٰٓ أَعْيُنِهِمْ فَٱسْتَبَقُوا۟ ٱلصِّرَٰطَ فَأَنَّىٰ يُبْصِرُونَ ﴿66﴾

Had We wished We would have blotted out their eyes: then, were they to advance towards the path, how would have they seen?

This verse and the two following verses are related to the previous verse regarding the testimony of the limbs.

Sometimes we question why God has given us all these bounties, means and powers, and then holds us responsible for them. One may sometimes wish they did not have these blessings and abilities so that they would not have responsibility for them too. The Qur'ān tells us that on the Day of Judgment people look at their actions being played back before their eyes, the rejecters will wish they were not created at all. 'The day when a person will observe what his hands have sent ahead and the faithless one will say, "I wish I were dust!"' (78:40) They wish they were not given any of these blessings.

Yet, what kind of creatures would we be if we did not have these blessings? We would not be able to find our way, fulfil our ambitions or fulfil our goal in life 'if had we wished we would have blotted out their eyes.' Here, *Tamasnā* means to wipe out completely so that no trace remains. It means God could have created humans with no trace of eyes or eye socket so that the eye was something unheard of.

How would have they seen; this sentence may mean that it was not possible for them to even imagine that they could not see, because they did not have any idea of vision. In fact, there may be many things in this world that we may not perceive or be ignorant of because we are not given the ability for that perception at all. There is no logical necessity that things in this world should be confined to our five means of perception.

$$\text{وَلَوْ نَشَاءُ لَمَسَخْنَٰهُمْ عَلَىٰ مَكَانَتِهِمْ فَمَا ٱسْتَطَٰعُوا۟ مُضِيًّا وَلَا يَرْجِعُونَ ﴿67﴾}$$

And had We wished We would have deformed them in their place; then they would neither have been able to move ahead nor to return.

If God wished, he could transform humans into motionless flesh. Our humanity (or human-ness) is a gift from God, yet it is through using these gifts that we defy him. He could have changed our creation in a way that rendered us paralysed and senseless. It is all by the power of his creation that these have become possible. Interestingly the following verse indicates that on reflection, this deformation happens to human beings in the later stages of their lives.

$$\text{وَمَن نُّعَمِّرْهُ نُنَكِّسْهُ فِى ٱلْخَلْقِ أَفَلَا يَعْقِلُونَ ﴿68﴾}$$

And whomever We give a long life, We cause him to regress in creation. Then, will they not exercise their reason?

The term *nunakkis* (we cause to regress) is derived from *tankīs* which means to reverse something in a manner that its top comes down and its bottom goes up. Here, it is used as a metonym for complete return of man to lack of knowledge, memory and power. 'There are some of you who are taken away by death, and there are some of you who are relegated to the nethermost age, so that he knows nothing after having possessed some knowledge.' (22:5)

This regression from vision to blindness, from hearing to deafness, from comprehension to dementia and amnesia is something that happens in our lifetime for many people. 'It is Allah who created you from weakness, then he gave you power after weakness. Then, after power, he ordained weakness and old age: he creates whatever he wishes, and he is the All-knowing, the All-powerful.' (30:54). He gradually takes back whatever he has given. If that is what God has destined due to aging, he could destine it any time in our life.

One other great wisdom that this verse teaches us is to limit our ambitions to a reasonable lifespan. After a certain age life has no value anymore. We have to shift our long-term ambitions to the life which is yet to come. The blessings of this life are time-limited. The real blessings which are not time-limited are yet to come:

> Worldly life may be compared to water we send down from the sky. It mingles with the plants of the earth on which mankind and

livestock feed until, when the earth takes on its trimmings and looks attractive, and its people think that they will be able to use them as they like, Our command comes along to it by night or daytime, and we mow it down ahead of time just as though it had not been so lush the day before. Thus, do we elaborate the signs for a people who reflect. Allah invites to the abode of peace, and he guides whomever he wishes to a straight path. (10:24-25)

وَمَا عَلَّمْنَـٰهُ ٱلشِّعْرَ وَمَا يَنۢبَغِى لَهُۥٓ إِنْ هُوَ إِلَّا ذِكْرٌ وَقُرْءَانٌ مُّبِينٌ ﴿69﴾

We did not teach him poetry, nor does it behoove him. This is just a reminder and a manifest Qur'ān,

---

This verse is returning to the theme set out in the beginning of the surah to substantiate the message so far. The opening verses stated that 'You are indeed one of the messengers on a straight path, with a scripture sent down from the All-mighty, the All-merciful, that you may warn a people whose fathers were not warned, so they are oblivious.' However, the rejecters accused him of fabricating his message and regarded him as a poet who could produce exceptional literature.

However, Allah refutes this saying by stating that, the messenger has not been able to produce a single line of poetry before this ('we did not teach him poetry'); secondly it does not behoove a messenger to recite poetry as poetry is based on imagination and emotion, while this text is based on knowledge and truth ('nor does it behoove him'), and thirdly, it is a reminder which can bring you knowledge of the unseen ('This is just a reminder and a manifest Qur'an').

The reason why the rejecters called the Prophet (s) a poet among other names such as a sorcerer, insane, a soothsayer, and a liar was that the Qur'an sounded like beautiful poetry. It was gentle, smooth and rhythmic; however, with a rhythm which had excelled every precedence and uniquely different from poetic rhymes. That is why when the master of poetry of Makkah, Walīd ibn Mughayrah was asked about his opinion regarding the Qur'ān, he said it did not sound like poetry and it was nothing but magic.

> Indeed, he reflected and decided. Perish he, how he decided! Again, perish he, how he decided! Then he looked; then he frowned and scowled. Then he went away disdainfully, saying, "It is nothing but magic handed down." (74:18-25)

An interesting fact about the Prophet (s) is that from birth to death, neither could he compose a line of poetry nor could he remember other people's poems; or at least he never recited a line of poetry composed by others. It is reported that sometimes the Prophet (s) tried to use a line of poetry to prove a point, but he could not remember it correctly and his companions had to correct him. This is the literal meaning of 'we did not teach him poetry,' although one may say that here the literal meaning is not intended and the verse simply means that the Qur'ān is not poetry.

The reason that Allah is so emphatic that the Qur'ān is not poetry is because poetry cannot be used for serious matters. Serious science, serious philosophy, and especially serious knowledge contained in the Qur'ān cannot be based on poetry, the essence of which is imagination and exaggeration. If the Qur'ān was poetry, one could say that all its concepts like Hell and Heaven, Resurrection and judgment, God and angels, were poetic imaginations. Therefore, the Qur'ān as a manifest book and as a reminder for mankind cannot be poetry.

لِّيُنذِرَ مَن كَانَ حَيًّا وَيَحِقَّ ٱلْقَوْلُ عَلَى ٱلْكَٰفِرِينَ ﴿70﴾

so that anyone who is alive may be warned, and that the word may come due against the faithless.

This verse outlines the purpose of the 'reminder and a manifest Qur'an': to warn whoever is alive and to inform the faithless that they will be subject to the decree of God. Clearly, the life mentioned in this verse is the life of the heart not life of the body. The Qur'ān regards those whose hearts are not impacted by admonition as dead. 'Indeed, you cannot make the dead hear, nor can you make the deaf hear the call when they turn their backs upon you.' (27:80) That is why many exegetes have interpreted *ḥayy* (alive) as *'āqil* (one who reflects).

Life can be classified to different levels. The first is the 'vegetative life,' which is the life making growth, nutrition, and reproduction possible. The second is the 'animal life,' which makes meaningful movement, emotions and feelings possible. The third is 'human life' which makes higher concepts, reflection, learning, receptiveness to admonition and advice, and spiritual connection possible. Each level entails the qualities of the lower levels. Therefore, a human being would have life in all three levels of vegetative, animal and human life. The Qur'ān regards the most important aspect of human life to be reflection, spiritual connection and receptiveness to admonition. That is why in this verse Allah says that the Qur'ān can only warn those who are alive, meaning only those who have human life in the sense mentioned.

In other verses, the Qur'ān regards many human beings as living only an animal life and depriving themselves of the highest level of life. 'Do you suppose that most of them listen or reflect? They are just like cattle; rather they are further astray from the way.' (25:44). As it is clear from this verse, what makes human life is the ability of 'listening' and 'reflecting':

> Certainly, we have created for Hell many of the *jinn* and humans: they have hearts with which they do not understand, they have eyes with which they do not see, they have ears with which they do not hear. They are like cattle; rather they are more astray. It is they who are the heedless. (7:179)

Animal life is driven by feelings, emotions and the satisfaction of bodily needs, while human life goes beyond those elementary matters. This is what the Qur'ān sometimes calls 'life of the heart.'

We can find many instances in *Nahj al-Balāghah* where Amīr al-Mu'minīn, Ali (a) emphasises the life of the heart, its diseases and its cures. In sermon 110, he says regarding the Qur'ān, '…and understand it thoroughly for it is the spring of the hearts, and seek cure in its light for verily it is the cure of the hearts.' In sermon 133 he says, 'Wisdom is a life for the dead hearts,' and he sometimes compares the sickness of the heart with the sickness of the body. In the aphorism 349 he says, 'He whose fear of Allah is less, his heart dies,' and in the aphorism 388 he says, 'Worse than bodily ailment is the disease of the heart.'

Thus, the phrase 'anyone who is alive may be warned' is talking about human life in its higher sense which is driven by reflection and spiritual contemplation. Those who are not driven by these faculties cannot be impacted; in fact, it is as if they do not hear at all. 'The parable of the faithless is that of someone who shouts after that which does not hear anything except a call and cry: they are deaf, dumb, and blind, they do not reflect.' (2:171)

And that the word may come due against the faithless; here 'faithless' is used as the antithesis of 'anyone who is alive.' So, the verse regards the faithless as dead in the sense mentioned above. The discussion of the phrase 'the word may come due against the faithless' took place during the commentary on verse seven. The conclusion was that the 'word' is the eternal decree of God which is explained in Surah al-Sajdah. 'Had we wished we would have given every soul its guidance, but I passed my just word: "Surely, I will fill Hell with all the [guilty] *jinn* and humans."' (32:13) It means that God has not willed to guide people by force, but by free will. The reason is that forced guidance does not result in placing man in the neighbourhood of God in Paradise. However, as God has willed to guide by free will, he has justly passed the 'word' to drive to Hell those who transgress and act arrogantly.

$$\text{أَوَلَمْ يَرَوْاْ أَنَّا خَلَقْنَا لَهُم مِّمَّا عَمِلَتْ أَيْدِينَآ أَنْعَٰمًا فَهُمْ لَهَا مَٰلِكُونَ ﴿71﴾}$$

Have they not seen that We have created for them—of what Our hands have worked—cattle, so they have become their masters?

For those who are alive and can reflect, some further signs of Allah are brought to their attention.

We have created for them - of what our hands have worked. This metaphorical expression signifies that everything in this world is made directly by God. Although there is that chain of causes and effects, and angels working hard behind the scene to make this world possible, these are all honorary mediums and everything is in reality 'worked' by his 'hand.' The same expression is used for the creation of Adam as well. 'He said, "O Iblīs, what prevented you from prostrating before what I have created with my own two hands?"'(38:75) So, everything created by his hands means that everything is created directly by him. If his hands, so to speak, are not at work the chain of causes would not work and the angels would be powerless. 'The Jews say, "Allah's hand is tied up." Tied up be their hands, and cursed be they for what they say! Rather, his hands are wide open: he bestows as he wishes.' (5:64) Without his hand being at work, the cattle would not give birth, the crops would not grow, the winds would not blow, and rain would not fall:

> It is he who sends the winds as harbingers of his mercy, and we send down from the sky purifying water, with which we revive a dead country and provide water to many of the cattle and humans we have created. (25:48-49)

...so they have become their masters?; A more fitting translation for this part would be 'And Lo! They own them.' This brings to our attention the expression 'which they own' which refers to Allah as the real owner of things. Only through his generosity do we become honorary owners of what in reality, belongs to him. He has made things in a way that they are submissive to us to the extent that we can possess them, and become their masters.

> وَذَلَّلْنَـٰهَا لَهُم فَمِنهَا رَكُوبُهُم وَمِنهَا يَأْكُلُونَ ﴿72﴾

> And We made them tractable for them; so some of them make their mounts and some of them they eat.

The camel, the horse and the cow, with their strength and power, are made tractable in a way that they can be used to ride on and to eat from them. They do not show resistance when we want to use them nor does their flesh poison our body. On the contrary their flesh is a means for our health and subsistence.

> وَلَهُم فِيهَا مَنَـٰفِعُ وَمَشَارِبُ أَفَلَا يَشكُرُونَ ﴿73﴾

> There are other benefits for them therein, and drinks. Will they not then give thanks?

Apart from eating and mounting, there are countless other benefits to be gained from cattle including: milk, wool, and leather. It is difficult to imagine life without cattle. That is probably why, among many different blessings surrounding us, some of which were mentioned in verses 33-44, here the Qur'an singles out the blessing of the cattle, because they are permanently present in our daily life; living without them requires a completely different diet and lifestyle. Even their droppings are used to fertilize the land and to make the trees more productive.

Will they not then give thanks? In return, what is expected from man is simply to be grateful. As mentioned before, gratefulness (*shukr*) has two pillars. The first is the acknowledgement of the blessing and the one who bestowed it in a way that creates reverence in the heart. The second is to use the blessing in a way that would not displease the one who bestowed it. Disobedience of God using the blessings he has bestowed on us is an open ungratefulness. A higher form of *shukr* is worship, which should be offered to God alone and not to any other, because whatever others give, in essence belong to God and are his blessings.

وَٱتَّخَذُواْ مِن دُونِ ٱللَّهِ ءَالِهَةً لَّعَلَّهُمْ يُنصَرُونَ ﴿74﴾

They have taken gods besides Allah, [hoping] that they might be helped [by the fake deities].

Ālihah (gods) is the plural of *ilāh*, which refers to someone worthy of worship. When we say *lā ilāha illa Allāh* we mean that there is nothing worthy of worship except Allah. As discussed above, worship is the highest expression of gratitude. As such, worshipping the creator is something rational, natural, and intuitive. Worshipping anything beside the creator is counter-intuitive, and irrational.

This verse explains that some people worship other beings in order to receive support and help from them. This type of worship is usually driven by superstition rather than an intuitive sense of gratitude. It is motivated by fear, worries, agonies and a sense of insecurity. It is because of this sense of insecurity and desertedness that people try to hold on to anything they imagine to be helpful; and to receive their help they start worshipping them. 'They take gods besides Allah hoping that they might be helped.'

That is why the essence of worship in monotheism is different from the essence of worship in polytheism. The former is driven by love and intuitive sense of gratitude while the latter is driven by bargaining worship for help and support.

لَا يَستَطِيعُونَ نَصرَهُم وَهُم لَهُم جُندٌ مُّحضَرُونَ ﴿75﴾

[Yet] they cannot help them, while they [themselves] are ready warriors for them.

[Yet] they cannot help them; this meaning is reiterated in countless places in the Qur'ān. Certainly, all power belongs to God or to whoever and whatever he authorizes:

Some people consider certain things equal to God and love them just as one should love God. However, the strongest of the believers' love is their love of God. Had the unjust been able to reflect about their condition, when facing the torment, they would have had no doubt that to God belongs All-power and that he is stern in his retribution. (2:165)

...while they [themselves] are ready warriors for them; The pronouns in this sentence allow two meanings. The idolaters will be a host brought up before the idols; or the idols will be a host brought up before the idolaters. However, both meanings imply one thing - they will be like armies standing against each other when the truth transpires. 'They have taken gods besides Allah that they may be a source of might to them. No Indeed! Soon they will disown their worship, and they will be their opponents.' (19:81-812)

The first meaning however, can be supported by further evidence from the Qur'ān. The idolaters will be a host brought up before the idols; this is another expression of 'The day we shall summon every group of people with their *imām*' (17:71), and if they have worshipped idols then their idols will be their leaders and they will be summoned up like a host for them. It may not be the physical idol but the concept that the idol represents. In any case, this is a serious threat. The idols are representation of *Iblīs* and *Shayātīn* who are bound to go to Hell, and if people are summoned as their hosts, they will go to Hell with them too.

The conversation between God and Satan is clear about it.

> Said he, "Do you see this one whom you have honoured above me? If you respite me until the Day of Resurrection, I will surely destroy his progeny, all except a few." Said he, "Begone! Whoever of them follows you, indeed the Hell shall be your requital, an ample reward." (17:62-63)

The same concept is addressed in Surah Maryam:

> Man says, "Shall I, when I have died, be brought forth alive?" Does not man remember that we created him before when he was nothing? By your Lord, we will surely gather them and the devils; then we will surely bring them up around Hell on their knees. (19:66-68)

How can people be the hosts or troops (*jund*) of the idols? The troops are usually the body of an army, those who support the cause of the leaders without having any say as to how and why the decisions are made. In our life, if we support a cause or an idea without having pondered upon it enough, we will become the troops of that cause; we will become the foot soldiers of that idea, and if the idea is a devilish one, then we will find ourselves when we will be resurrected as the *jund* of that devil. Whoever supports or enhances or puts forward an argument of Satan or a satanic cause or concept, on the Day of Judgment will be a troop of Satan and will follow him to Hell.

We are loose troops of many ideas in our lifetimes; sometimes we support godly concepts and sometimes satanic concepts, but we must be careful that we do not follow so many satanic concepts that we become part of his troops on the Resurrection Day. In Surah al-Shu'arā there is a heart rendering allusion to the pitiful situation of these troops on the Day of Judgment:

> The day when neither wealth nor children will avail, except him who comes to Allah with a sound heart, and Paradise will be brought near for the God wary, and Hell will be brought into view for the perverse, and they shall be told: "Where is that which you used to worship besides Allah? Do they help you, or can they help each other?" Then they will be cast into it on their faces they and the perverse, and the hosts of Iblīs all together. They will say, as they

wrangle in it with each other, "By Allah, we had indeed been in manifest error, when we equated you with the Lord of all the worlds! And no one led us astray except the guilty. Now we have no intercessors, nor do we have any sympathetic friend." (26:88-101)

Thus, we have to be very careful about the concepts and causes we support in this world.

Sometimes Muslims follow satanic causes, without realising it. We have to pray to God that in the business of our lives we do not support such causes. They may seem to be very idyllic and nice at first glance, but under their veneer they are satanic and make us members of Satan's party. 'Satan has dominated them and has made them forget the guidance of God. They are Satan's party and the party of Satan will certainly suffer a great loss.' (58:19)

﴿فَلَا يَحْزُنكَ قَوْلُهُمْ إِنَّا نَعْلَمُ مَا يُسِرُّونَ وَمَا يُعْلِنُونَ ﴿76﴾

So do not let their remarks grieve you. We indeed know whatever they hide and whatever they disclose.

So do not let their remarks grieve you; Refusal of the truth is always a saddening and upsetting situation, especially if it is by your closest friends, relatives, and loved ones. For the Prophet (s), however, it was not only the rejection that hurt, but the remarks and accusations were heart breaking. Some of those remarks are quoted in the Qur'ān:

> The faithless say, "This is nothing but a lie that he has fabricated, and other people have abetted him in it." Thus, they have certainly come out with wrongdoing and falsehood. They say, "he has taken down myths of the ancients, and they are dictated to him morning and evening." (25:4-5)

> And they say, "What sort of apostle is this who eats food and walks in the marketplaces? Why has not an angel been sent down to him so as to be a warner along with him?" Or, "Why is not a treasure thrown to him, or why does he not have a garden from which he may eat?" And the wrongdoers say, "You are just following a bewitched man." (25:6-8)

In other places, they accused him of being soothsayer, a sorcerer, a poet, and insane.

We indeed know whatever they hide and whatever they disclose; This is a consolation for the Prophet (s) reassuring him that they do not say or plot anything openly or secretly except that Allah knows of it and will take care of it. Their plots and accusations are known by Allah even before coming to their minds.

أَوَلَمْ يَرَ ٱلْإِنسَٰنُ أَنَّا خَلَقْنَٰهُ مِن نُّطْفَةٍ فَإِذَا هُوَ خَصِيمٌ مُّبِينٌ ﴿77﴾

Does not man see that We created him from a drop of [seminal] fluid, and, behold, he is an open contender!?

Mujāhid, 'Ikrimah, and Qatadah have reported that a man named Ubayy bin Khalaf (or 'Ās ibn Wā'il according to Ibn Abbas), came to the Prophet (s) with a dry bone in his hand, which he was crumbling and scattering in the air. He said, 'O Muhammad! Are you claiming that Allah will resurrect this?' The Prophet (s) said, 'Yes, Allah, the exalted, will cause you to die, then he will resurrect you and will gather you into the Fire.' At that occasion, this verse and the following verses until the end of surah was revealed.

Nuṭfah (drop of fluid) originally means a small amount of water. In the Qur'ān, it is usually used for seminal water. The argument is very clear: man who was created from a drop of water, to a clinging mass, to a fleshy tissue, to a foetus, to a baby, to a human, now argues with his creator. In fact, the Qur'ān takes the very process of our creation as a proof for resurrection:

O people! If you are in doubt about the resurrection, consider that we indeed created you from dust, then from a drop of seminal fluid, then from a clinging mass, then from a fleshy tissue, partly formed and partly unformed, so that we may manifest [Our power] to you. We establish in the wombs whatever we wish for a specified term, then we bring you forth as infants, then we rear you so that you may come of age. Then there are some of you who are taken away, and there are some of you who are relegated to the nethermost age, so that he knows nothing after having possessed some knowledge. And you see the earth torpid, yet when we send down water upon it, it stirs and swells, and grows every delightful kind of plant. (22:5)

...he is an open contender; there is a subtle delicacy in this expression in that, on the one hand, it acknowledges the ingenious capabilities of man while, on the other hand it condemns the way he uses those capabilities.

From one side, it acknowledges the inherent intelligence, intellect, understanding, independent will, authority, and power placed in that drop of water, but on the other side, it condemns his vainglory, forgetfulness of his origin, and ungratefulness to his

Lord, to the extent that he uses all the blessings given to him against the one who bestows those blessings and disputes with his creator.

وَضَرَبَ لَنَا مَثَلاً وَنَسِيَ خَلْقَهُ قَالَ مَن يُحْيِي ٱلْعِظَامَ وَهِىَ رَمِيمٌ ﴿78﴾

He draws comparisons for Us, and forgets his own creation. He says, 'Who shall revive the bones when they have decayed?'

Creation of every single human being is a miracle in itself. It is enough of a miracle that we see a drop of fluid after ten or fifteen years become a rational entity with all those faculties, feelings, emotions, thoughts, speech. It just needs a little contemplation about ourselves; however, the problem is that we forget our own creation. Man forgets about himself, that Allah created him from an insignificant fluid and brought him into existence from nothing.

When 'Ubay ibn Khalaf finds a rotten bone in the desert and brings it to the Prophet (s), crushes it into powder, then scatters it in the air saying, "Who can give life to this rotten bone?" he is certain he will not receive any logical answer for his objection. He thought he had the firmest of all proofs. But all his argument collapses by the simple rejoinder, 'he forgets his own creation.'

We only need to look around ourselves to see that 'God has power over everything.' (2:259). Sometimes people wonder how is it possible to have all those wondrous things in Paradise, as described in the Qur'ān and the narrations. To them, it cannot be real; it is unimaginable. Well, what we see in this world was unimaginable when we were in the wombs of our mothers. Through bearing witness to the power of God in the present plane in which we live we have to understand that God has power over everything. 'Certainly, you have known the first genesis, then why do you not take admonition?' (56:62).

قُلْ يُحْيِيهَا ٱلَّذِيٓ أَنشَأَهَآ أَوَّلَ مَرَّةٍ وَهُوَ بِكُلِّ خَلْقٍ عَلِيمٌ ﴿79﴾

Say, 'He will revive them who produced them the first time, and He has knowledge of all creation.

If this bone and all other human and animal limbs, organs, minds and hearts, were made from an insignificant droplet of water, which was made from dust, which in its turn was made out of nothing, it is clear that its creator is able to bring rotten bones back to life again.

He has knowledge of all creation. This sentence can have two meanings. One is that he has the knowledge of creating anything that he wants. By looking around us we realise the truth of this claim. He has created whatever he has wished out of atoms and cells. He has created huge and tiny creatures as big as the heavens and the earth and as small as unicellular organisms.

The other meaning of the verse is that he has knowledge of all created beings. Thus, scattered pieces of crumbled bones do not escape his knowledge and he can gather them and bring them together for resurrection. An unbeliever asked Imam al-Ṣādiq (a), 'How can individuals be resurrected when their bodies have decayed or been consumed by wild animals and insects, or become part of the soil and made into bricks for building walls?' The Imam (a) replied: 'The one who created them from nothing and fashioned them without a previous mould is capable of bringing them back to existence, just as he did the first time.' The man asked for further details. The Imam (a) said:

> The souls exist in their own specific locations. The souls of the righteous are in a place of light and spaciousness, while the souls of the corrupt are in a place of darkness and narrowness. At the same time, the body disintegrates into the earth from which it originated. Everything

that was consumed and excreted by animals and insects is preserved in the ground in the knowledge of God, who is aware of the size and weight of every cell in the depths of the earth. The cells of sentient beings are like gold nuggets which are distinct from the rocks and soil that surrounds them, or like lumps of butter that become separate from milk. Thereafter, the cells of each being will come together and with God's permission, proceed towards the place where their soul is located. With the permission of the Fashioner, all the bodies will reassume their former features, and the souls will once again occupy them. In this way, the individual is once again complete and self-aware.

In another *hadīth* Imam al-Ṣādiq (a) further explains

The bodies of beings who possess a soul will be scattered as dust within the ground like gold amongst common rocks. When the resurrection occurs, it will rain so heavily that it will disturb the ground. Then, just as gold is sifted from soil, human dust will break free from the earth around them and assemble.

This means that cells that once possessed life shall eternally maintain their identity and once conditions are favourable, they will easily separate from the other elements around them. Thereafter, according to the rules that God has ordained for that Day, the dispersed cells of every human being will come together and reassemble. Of course, not all the cells may be available as they may have been consumed and become parts of other humans, that is why new cells are added to what has remained. Imam al-Ṣādiq explains in another *hadīth*, 'When God wills to resurrect the human beings, he will cause it to rain for forty days during which time their bones will gather and flesh will form over them.'

ٱلَّذِى جَعَلَ لَكُم مِّنَ ٱلشَّجَرِ ٱلْأَخْضَرِ نَارًا فَإِذَآ أَنتُم مِّنْهُ تُوقِدُونَ ﴿80﴾

He, who made for you fire out of the green tree, and, behold, you light fire from it!

This is another example of how God can create things that the ordinary human mind considers impossible. He is the one who initiated the creation of trees from water, then they become green and beautiful, bearing fruit, then he develops it until the tree becomes dry wood with which fires are lit. What begins as water ends up as fire. Producing fire from firewood, though usually taken for granted, is one of the most essential amenities of life, and it comes from a substance which is essentially made of water and soil neither of which is combustible. This is sufficient proof that Allah can do whatever he wills and he can create however he wishes. God can certainly bring life back to dead bodies.

Some commentators have suggested another interpretation for this verse. It is reported from Ibn Abbas that this verse refers to the Markh and the 'Afār trees, which grow in Hijāz. If two branches of these trees are rubbed together, they can create a fire without kindling. So, they are just like kindling, but the fire is produced from green trees rather than dry wood. The argument is that the Lord, who can bring out fire from these green trees, is also able to give life to the dead; as water and fire are two opposites. The one who can put them beside each other has the ability to bring forth life and death.

$$\text{أَوَلَيْسَ ٱلَّذِى خَلَقَ ٱلسَّمَٰوَٰتِ وَٱلْأَرْضَ بِقَٰدِرٍ عَلَىٰٓ أَن يَخْلُقَ مِثْلَهُم بَلَىٰ وَهُوَ ٱلْخَلَّٰقُ ٱلْعَلِيمُ ﴿81﴾}$$

Is not He who created the heavens and the earth able to create the like of them? Yes indeed! He is the All-creator, the All-knowing.

This is another compelling proof for resurrection to a new life. The one who created life once, can create it again. The one who set up this firmament can do it again.

The nature of pronoun used in 'create the like of them' '(*yakhluqa mithlahum*) means that it does not refer to Heavens and the earth because the pronoun *hum* is only used for intelligent beings. So, the creation of the Heavens and the earth and the knowledge and power that it involves is brought to our attention to show that God can create the like of humans again when he gives life to the dead. This is mentioned explicitly in Surah al-Aḥqāf, 'Do they not see that Allah, who created the Heavens and the earth and who was not exhausted by their creation, is able to revive the dead? Yes, indeed he has power over all things.' (46:33)

Some commentators have raised a question here. Are we going to come back on the Day of Judgment identically as we are now today or, is it a similar being that comes back? The question here is concerned with giving life to the rotten bones. There is no issue with the idea that the human soul will come to life in the identical way that they left this world. However, the human body undergoes a constant process of growth and transformation; cells die and are replaced by other cells on a daily basis.

Although we are the same person we were last month, our bodies are not the same bodies they were last month, or even the same as last night. We have many cells that have died, and many cells that have replaced them. Often, we are negligent of small changes, but even the appearance of the body changes every year. We cannot say we have the same body we had last year or last week. Thus, when life is given back to the rotten bones of the body, it is difficult to decipher which body will return. It could be our old bodies, or young bodies. Thus, we have to conclude that although the soul comes back in the same form as the moment we died, the body will be like this body with new cells. Bodies which still have the fingerprints of our body in this world. That is why we can recognise each other.

In this world too, we can recognise each other although our bodies are constantly changing. Even if we see different pictures of the same person; from different points in their life, from childhood pictures to wedding photos, the person can be easily identified as the same person in both pictures, but in physical reality they are not because the physique and body have changed. So, although our bodies are recreated from the remaining cells of our bones, they are not exactly the same. This is probably what the expression 'able to create the like of them' signifies.

He is the All-creator, the All-knowing. The creativity of Allah is something which has perplexed philosophers and people of intelligence. No one has ever produced a satisfactory answer to explain how God creates and when he started to create, although this last question is paradoxical in itself because he is the creator of the time and *when* too. Over the past thousands of years, mystics and philosophers, each with their own language and interpretations have tried to answer this question, but none have come up with an answer that satisfies human beings in this regard. It is a secret bigger than the human mind, perception and comprehension. There is however, an explanation in the Qurʾān which is expressed in the following verse, although it may lead to more questions than answers.

إِنَّمَا أَمْرُهُ إِذَا أَرَادَ شَيْئًا أَنْ يَقُولَ لَهُ كُنْ فَيَكُونُ ﴿82﴾

All His command, when He wills something, is to say to it 'Be,' and it is.

The main claim of this verse is that God does not need any means in creation. He does not need to think, plan, nor does he need to seek any means, medium or raw material. When he wills something he just says 'Be and it is.'

In the first sermon of *Nahj al-Balāghah*, Imam Ali explains:

He initiated creation in a fascinating way; he

commenced it originally, without reflection of thought, or use of experience, or need of movement, or agitation of mind. He allotted all things their times, put together their variations, gave them their properties, and determined their features knowing them before creating them, realising fully their limits and confines and knowing their propensities and intricacies."

God does not create like we make things. He has only a will, expressed here as a command. And even that will, is his creation, as Imam Ali (a) explains in sermon 186, 'When he intends to create something he just says '"Be" and it is but not through a voice that strikes (the ears) or a call that could be heard. His speech is an act that he creates.'

It is true that the more this is explored the more confusing it becomes, because this is a realm which our intellect cannot reach. 'Imagination cannot reach him to assign him quantity. Understanding cannot think of him to give him quality. Senses do not perceive him to grasp him.' (Sermon 186)

Therefore, to bring the dead to life, he simply needs to will it. For him easy and difficult have no meaning. Easy and difficult are compared with the amount of available power, means and knowledge; for one who has infinite knowledge and power, ease and difficulty are irrelevant. That is why in interpreting the verse 'It is he who originates the creation, and then he will bring it back and that is easier for him.' (30:27) all exegetes agree that it is easier for him in our comparison of the two, because for God nothing is easier or more difficult. Even time has no meaning in his creation. Time is a dimension that he gives to his creation not that he spends to create. It does not take him time to create things, but he creates things and gives them time. 'It is he who created you from clay, then decreed a fixed time for you.' (6:2) So, it is as he says, 'All that we say to a thing, when we will it, is to say to it "Be!" And it is.' (16:40)

فَسُبْحَٰنَ ٱلَّذِى بِيَدِهِ مَلَكُوتُ كُلِّ شَىْءٍ وَإِلَيْهِ تُرْجَعُونَ

﴿83﴾

So immaculate is He in whose hand is the dominion of all things, and to whom you shall be brought back.

SubḥanAllāh is a sentence with an implicit verb, either in imperative or indicative case. The full sentence would be *sabbiḥ subḥanAllāh* or *usabbiḥu subḥanAllāh*. They mean respectively 'purify (or glorify) the way Allah should be purified', or 'I purify the way Allah should be purified'. In Arabic grammar, *subḥāna* is the qualifying object (*maf'ūli muṭlaq*).

Purifying God means that we negate any defect, shortcoming, inability, or any imperfection from him. Depending on the context, this may be a specific imperfection or inability. In this verse since the context is about giving life back to the dead, it implies that he is above any inability to bring them back, since the dominion of all things is in his hand. Here, 'he in whose hand is the dominion of all things,' is a title which signifies the reason for his immaculateness.

He in whose hand is the dominion of all things; dominion is a translation for *malakūt*. The Qur'ān introduces two different orders of kingdom for God's power and dominion. One is *mulk* and the other is *malakūt*. The latter is used in this verse. The former can be found in many verses, for example in Surah al-Mulk (Dominion), 'Blessed is he in whose hand is the kingdom (*mulk*), and he has power over all things.' (67:1) Also, in Surah al-Ḥadīd, 'His is the kingdom (*mulk*) of the Heavens and the earth he gives life and causes death and he has power over all things.' (57:2) English translations usually translate *mulk* as kingdom or sovereignty, and *malakūt* as sovereignty or dominion or kingdom. However, they have different meanings. Although, both of these terms refer to the kingdom of God, they signify different levels of sovereignty as it appears to us.

The *mulk* is the corporeal realm, also known as the observable universe that we understand. Everything is conducted by his measurement and design, the chain of causes and effects is working by his blessing, and nothing escapes his power and knowledge. This is a great kingdom; however, God's sovereignty is greater and deeper than that. The level of *malakūt* is the spiritual realm also known as the intellectual realm, where the spiritual faculties reside. There, everything is seen to be directly dependent on him, the chain of causes and effects seems to be just an illusion there, and everything individually and directly is seen to be held by God. If people can see that dominion then all doubts would disperse and nothing but the truth is witnessed.

This dominion is what Allah showed Prophet Ibrahim (a) and his close friends. 'Thus, did we show Abraham the dominions (*malakūt*) of the Heavens and the earth, that he might be of those who possess certitude.' (6:75) Every atom, cell, object and living soul has a *mulki* aspect and a *malakūti* aspect. The *mulki* aspect manifests the wise design, fascinating creation as a sign of God, and the *malakūti* aspect manifests their inseparable dependence and reliance on and sustenance by God. As such, this verse is an excellent closing for the surah and all its remarks.

And to whom you shall be brought back; We are being taken on a journey the destination of which is meeting with the Lord. 'O man! You are labouring toward your Lord laboriously, and you will encounter him.' (83:6) It means we are gathering spiritual strength stage after stage, and grow at each station of the journey, until we are capable for the great encounter.

Everything before that encounter, before *ākhira*, is a journey that we are taken through. We began as dust, became water, then an embryo, then we came into the world, and then we shall leave it; we will thereafter travel along until we will reach *ākhira*, where we will rest for eternity, 'The hereafter (*ākhira*) is the home of permanent settlement.' (40:39) Real life and meaningful existence is only possible when we reach our destination, when we return to God. What we experience in this world is a pale shadow and fleeting fragrance of life in comparison to what is to come.

Compared to that, the life of this world is no more than play and sport, which prepares us for the real life that is to follow; 'And the life of this world is nothing more than diversion and play! And the abode of the Hereafter is indeed life, if only they knew.' (29:64) *Ākhira* is the culmination of the hierarchy of existence; a world which has developed from primitive beginnings to an unimaginable level of perfection, just as a tiny oak develops into a strong oak tree. As Jesus

(a) is reported to have said in the Gospel of Matthew (13:32):

> Things in the realm of dominion of God (*malakūt*) are like a mustard seed planted in a field. The mustard seed is the tiniest of seeds, yet it matures into a bush that is bigger than others. It becomes as big as a tree and birds nest in its branches.

Remembrance and reverence of God in this world are like seeds which grow and elevate the potential of man to bear the fruits of hereafter:

> Do you not consider how God makes up a parable? A good word is like a good tree: its roots are steady and its branches are in the sky. It gives its fruit every moment by the leave of its Lord. God draws these parables for mankind so that they may take admonition. (14:24-25)

On the other hand, egoism and self-centredness kill human potential in a way that removes our harmony with the rest of the creation and makes us act foolishly in dissonance with everything else. If we wish to live in harmony with the rest of creation and progress into the next stage of our existence with peace and contentment we have to take away our attention from our lower selves and direct it towards the creator of all things. To whom we 'shall be brought back'.

This brings us to the end of the surah, and what a beautiful ending. The surah began by a mention of the straight path revealed to us by the Almighty God, took us through a tour of history, brought to our attention different sets of Allah's blessings, described for us the journey ahead, and eventually brought us to acknowledge his dominion and our involuntary journey back to him. 'And the terminus is toward your Lord' (53:42).

www.ingramcontent.com/pod-product-compliance
Lightning Source LLC
Chambersburg PA
CBHW021056080526
44587CB00010B/259